Whiskey Lore's Travel Guide To

EXPERIENCING IRISH WHISKEY

Learn • Plan • Taste • Tour

by

Drew Hannush

ISBN: 978-1-7348651-3-4
Kindle ISBN: 978-1-7348651-4-1

DEDICATION

To all the passionate owners, distillers, ambassadors, and tour guides who took the time to help me discover an island filled with fascinating spirits.

I came to Ireland looking to discover the story of Irish whiskey. I left filled with excitement for the spirits to come and friendships to last a lifetime.

Here's to you. *Sláinte maith!*

Table of Contents

Introduction

IN SEARCH OF IRISH WHISKEY

If you had asked me a couple of years ago what my next travel book would be about, Irish whiskey distilleries would probably have been the last thing on my list.

The stage seemed set. I had already followed up my trip to Kentucky bourbon country with two trips to Scotland for my blog Travel Fuels Life. During those journeys I visited over 40 scotch distilleries. And although my first trip to Scotland included four days driving around southern Ireland, it was my opinion that Ireland was for beer and Scotland was for whisky. While I made it to one Irish distillery on that trip, I left with the impression that Ireland's whiskey industry only had a handful of distilleries versus at least 140 in Scotland. It hardly appeared worthy of a travel guide.

While planning a trip with my sister to Barcelona in 2019, I pondered adding Scotland to my itinerary, especially since I would already be on that side of the Atlantic. I don't remember what prompted me to look up Irish distilleries but, when I looked, I was surprised to find a dozen that offered tours.

I thought, hey, I could include this as part of my current itinerary and if it was worthy of a book, I would write one. If not, then my consolation prize would be a trip around Ireland. I booked the flights and reserved my lodgings.

THE TIME FOR IRISH WHISKEY IS NOW

One thing I have learned through my years of travel is to prepare for the unexpected. With the trip just a month away and anticipation growing, I suddenly found myself forced to cancel the entire itinerary. It was March 2020 and we all know what happened then.

The next year and a half halted all of my international whiskey travel and kept me mostly in Kentucky and Tennessee. But, as the calendar turned to 2022 and the world opened up, Ireland was once again calling.

Being a diligent researcher, I compared my 2020 list of Irish distilleries with other lists that might show some new entries in the whiskey landscape.

My jaw dropped!

Suddenly my spreadsheet of distilleries took on a life of its own. Names like Killowen, Old Carrick Mill, Lough Gill, Killarney, and Clonakilty seemed to appear out of nowhere. I also bumped into a sizable collection of unfamiliar brand names such as Hyde, Lambay, McConnell's, Natterjack, and Glendalough that warranted investigation. Others appeared to have distillery experiences in the works, like Powerscourt, Echlinville, and Skellig Six18.

What started as an 'excuse me' trip to Ireland was turning into a major adventure and a fantastic opportunity. How often do you get to see an entire whiskey industry rejuvenating itself right before your eyes?

Yet there was a problem. How would I craft a travel guide to an Irish whiskey landscape that was still emerging?

With Kentucky, I could buy my own tickets and give an unbiased view of the standard tour. With Ireland, some distilleries had tours, but many did not. I could wait three years for tours to develop. But there seemed to be so many interesting ones to visit now, with more opening in the next year or two. I wanted people to have the same special opportunity to discover this emerging industry as I had.

I decided the best strategy was to go behind the scenes and get to know the Irish whiskey industry up-close and personal. I sought founders, distillers, and ambassadors so I could ask about the scope of current or future tours. I wanted to find out when they filled their first barrel with new make, so readers could get a sense of when the distillery might have non-sourced whiskeys.

I took my spreadsheet and planned the most ambitious schedule of my life. My goal was to visit at least 45 distilleries in 24 days. I began plotting out the trip on Google Maps, using my experiences of past distillery travel in Scotland and Kentucky. Then I considered bed and breakfasts, food stops, money management, and fueling options to make my trip as worry free as possible.

As soon as the plan took shape, I contacted the distilleries, set dates, booked my flights, and locked in my lodgings.

When I reached out to the distilleries, it heartened me to hear how excited they were to host me. It truly is an industry that is primed for tourists. But it also surprised me when a couple of distillery owners questioned how many legitimate distilleries there really were in Ireland. After years of one monopoly running all of Irish whiskey, there was still a feeling that most of these brands were just bonders (companies that mature, blend, and bottle whiskey) and had no intention of distilling their own spirits. I could see that this book would open the eyes of not only travelers, but the industry itself.

Once I arrived in Ireland, it only took a handful of distillery visits before I started moving past all the stereotypes I had heard about Irish whiskey. I learned that not all Irish whiskey is triple distilled, it isn't all blends, it isn't all designed to be smooth, and not every distillery spells whiskey with an "e." Much of the narrative we know is thanks to the monopoly that controlled Irish whiskey for generations. With the growth of the industry, these accepted norms are being challenged by an island filled with creative distillers.

As my travels progressed, I realized just how historic this journey was. Not since the 1880s, when English writer Alfred Barnard traveled through Ireland and documented 29 of its distilleries, has anyone seen this many distilleries during a single trip. And, amazingly, I found even more distilleries in the development phase. If Barnard's work captured the moment when Irish was the most prized whiskey in the world, I was capturing the rebirth of that distilling empire.

The people are amazing, the spirits intriguing, the stories and histories fantastic, and the landscape between each distillery is incredible. In three and a half weeks, I went from the ranks of the Irish whiskey curious to an Irish whiskey believer.

WHY YOU WILL LOVE TOURING IRISH DISTILLERIES

If I were a betting man, I would say convincing you of this won't be too difficult.

There is mystery in the emerging world of Irish whiskey. New brands are joining Jameson, Bushmills, the Spots, and Redbreast on store shelves. And for the first time, you may now see an Irish whiskey section in your favorite liquor store, with unfamiliar styles like single grain and single pot still standing alongside traditional blends. If you are like me, those labels will be piquing your curiosity, with their Irish imagery, Gaelic-sounding names and icons, and historical references. Some of these bottles tell a story while others beckon you through engaging packaging.

Yet, through all of this, you are only at a marketing-level view of what lies behind the label. The experience of your favorite Irish whiskey isn't complete without obtaining a genuine sense of where it came from. After touring a distillery, I promise you these whiskeys will take on a whole new personality.

You will see the stunning copper pot stills and learn how their shapes and designs enhance the whiskey you love. You will understand processes that make a whiskey unique. You will hear the reason the distillery created it. You will see the barrels they store it in—you might even get to draw some out with what is called a whiskey thief. There will be a comradery on the tour as you speak with fellow whiskey travelers. You will pick up scents, flavors, and sensations through a guided tasting that will change how you experience whiskey from that day forward.

The first distillery I visited raised my whiskey IQ by leaps and bounds. I learned what whiskey is; I could see beyond the marketing and sensed what the distillery took pride in. I heard stories of how the founders chose the name of the distillery and its brands. I tasted whiskey finished in different barrel types. I took in a deep breath of the warehouse's sweet vapors—known as the angel's share—and marveled at the sheer amount of whiskey they had in storage. I learned what new make is and had my first taste. I gained a deeper understanding of Irish culture, history, and its influence on the world.

And I left with a second layer of questions, like are cows really happier because they eat the distillery's spent grains? Or was the distillery I visited really the oldest, as they claimed? It was a fantastic experience, and it made me excited for my next whiskey adventure.

You would think that after visiting hundreds of distilleries I would be sick of hearing about the process of making whiskey. But each distillery I visited had a different way of presenting it, and there were so many layers that I caught something new each time. It is fun to detect the subtle differences.

I don't expect you to visit as many distilleries as I did on my trip—I go a little overboard when I get into research mode. But this book will definitely help you plan a trip near that size, if you so choose. But it will also be an invaluable guide if all you can do is visit one Irish distillery.

My promise to you is that after reading this book, you will have:

- Gained the expertise you need to plan out the logistics of an Irish whiskey tour of Ireland and Northern Ireland.
- A deeper knowledge of what to expect from your distillery visits, including how to approach the tastings.
- A strong foundational Irish whiskey education so you will know what to listen for on your tours.
- A fun and relaxed time when you go to Ireland, knowing that you picked out the perfect selection of distilleries for your trip.

I hope you have such a great time that you feel compelled to reach out to me on *facebook.com/whiskeylore* or *instagram.com/whiskeylore* and that you tell me all the best parts of your trip.

After touring Ireland myself, I am no longer curious. I am an Irish whiskey fan. The level of creativity on this island is incredible and the people are passionate believers in what they are distilling. It's amazing to think how much of this journey I would have missed if I had visited two years earlier; the diversity and selection on the island has grown exponentially.

So if you are ready to take the plunge, let this be your guide to planning out your very first Irish whiskey journey. If you still aren't sure whether Irish whiskey is something you should dive into, let this book educate you on where the spirit came from, where it is now, and where it is going. If you just want to widen your knowledge about those whiskeys being added to your store shelves, use this book as your education and reference tool to all that is Irish whiskey. And if you love seeing an industry on the rise, hang onto this book and compare it to future editions, to see how the dreams of today turn into the whiskey empires of tomorrow.

Like the Emerald Isle itself, Irish whiskey gives us plenty of room to explore. It helps us open our senses. It connects us to the proud men and women who create the spirit. It ties directly to the history and culture of the Irish people. And it creates a wonderful conversation piece. Best of all, in a world that seems divided, it unites us in one big happy family of whiskey enthusiasts.

How To Use This Book

When I write these travel guides, I want them to be empowering resources. What I don't want to do is create a book full of my own opinions and rankings. There are a couple of reasons for this:

First, we all have different reasons for taking this journey, and every distillery I visit has its own distinct offerings and personality. Who am I to judge what may or may not appeal to you? Maybe you like history, or you want to know the science behind the spirits. Perhaps you have a passion for a brand, or you heard a story about someone or something associated with that distillery and that alone is enough to capture your interest. Each distillery is great in its own way. I want you to judge for yourself.

Second, if I tell you everything there is to know about the distillery, I am taking away the fun of learning these things for yourself as you take the tour.

So, the first part of the book is to help give you a solid foundation of information. I'll start with a high-level view of the history of Irish whiskey, then I'll tell you the basics of distilling, introduce some terms you will hear on your tours, and I'll help you spot marketing versus substance.

I want you to have an easy time planning out your trip, so in the next part I will guide you through important considerations like whether to hire a tour guide, how much of the country to cover, or how to choose the right size or style of distillery. I'll even help you focus on regions and options for transportation and lodging.

For those that are new to whiskey or who want to understand how to approach the tasting portion of your tours, I have created a section that will give you tips on how to taste whiskey, the type of glass you might invest in, and the ins and outs of nosing and detecting flavor notes. I'll even give you some insider tips on the flavors to expect, from the name of the style.

With this solid footing, you will gain the expertise you need to put together your own Irish whiskey itinerary. This is where the last section of the book becomes an invaluable resource. You will find all the critical information you need to pick out the distilleries that are right for you. There are around 50 whiskey distilleries in Ireland and here you can find out which ones currently have tours, which are coming soon, and which require a longer wait. From there, you can shorten your list to the ones you most want to visit, so there are fewer websites to review during your initial planning.

The profiles of distilleries with tours include maps, the focus of the tour, the brands of whiskey made there, what days the tours run, how to get there, special considerations, side trips, and suggestions for the next closest distilleries. In addition, I have written descriptions for each of the distilleries that are coming soon, including their web addresses. There is also a handy brand index in the back of the book, so you can find distilleries by the brand names you know and love.

Once you determine your ultimate collection of distilleries, you can use the links listed in the profiles to see interactive maps or book tours yourself. Or head to **whiskey-lore.com/signup**, fill in the form for a free membership, and enter the promo code **withorwithoute**. This code will allow you full access to our online Irish distillery tour-planning guide, including a time-saving distillery wish list feature.

Have fun putting together your incredible journey but always remember...

BE RESPONSIBLE.

The greatest joy in sipping whiskey is discovering its hidden depths and character. If you're looking to escape reality or crave the feeling of getting drunk, this book is not for you. But, if you are curious about whiskey and want to discover the pleasures of tasting, analyzing and discovering the amazing flavors and smells Irish whiskeys offer, or if you love experiencing the tradition and history of distilleries, then you've come to the right place.

Welcome and enjoy. And as the Irish say:

Sláinte (pronounced SLAHN-che)—to your health.

Part 1: Understanding Irish Whiskey

PART ONE

UNDERSTANDING IRISH WHISKEY

~~~~~~~~~~~~~~~~~~~~

"What whiskey will not cure, there is no cure for."

Irish Proverb

PART 1
Understanding Irish Whiskey

You may ask yourself, "why do I need to learn about Irish whiskey before I go on a trip to learn about Irish whiskey?" That is an excellent question, and I believe I have a worthy answer.

Have you ever enjoyed a movie so much that you went to see it a second time? When you watched it through again, did you notice dialogue and situations that you missed the first time?

As humans, our brains are always active. While processing the things that are happening, we also try to figure out what might happen next. The second time you watch a movie, your brain stops charging ahead, relaxes, and allows you to notice additional detail.

This chapter will focus on giving you a good baseline of knowledge, so that your brain isn't constantly trying to process what was just said while the tour guide charges on to the next subject. Each distillery will have its own history and special way of producing whiskey, and I want you to catch these unique details. I will help you understand what to listen for and what the jargon means.

And then there is the marketing. Not everything you hear on a distillery tour is a proven fact. Marketing sometimes leans too much on the legends and myths. It can also get caught up in the trap of brand or industry exuberance. In this section, you will learn to beware of words like "best" and "oldest." These are words that have a lot of caveats or stretch the truth to its very limits. And by the time you reach your third distillery, you may catch conflicting stories. I'll help clarify these things ahead of time, so you can be more present during your journey.

Let's jump right into the most important question of all:

WHAT IS IRISH WHISKEY?

Irish whiskey is a whiskey that comes from Ireland, right? How hard can it be? Well, there is a lot more to it than just that. And here we find our first marketing myths.

During my tours of Irish distilleries, I heard guides telling visitors that Irish whiskey is always triple distilled, it isn't smoky like scotch, and it has to be aged three years and a day. And since scotch is only aged for three years, that extra day makes Irish whiskey better. Now, I know some tour guides say this last bit to get a chuckle, but I have also seen it said with a straight face.

In reality, there are plenty of double-distilled Irish whiskeys and, as long as the warehouse manager can keep the spirit over 40% alcohol by volume after it has aged, you could even single distill it. As for smokiness, not all distilleries in Scotland use peat and there may soon be a couple of distilleries in Ireland that will exclusively use peat (or turf as it is called in Ireland). As for that "three years and a day" story, the Irish are not alone in providing this comic relief; I have heard Scottish tour guides tell the same fable.

Where did these stereotypes come from? Many of them developed out of the brilliant marketing of one company, Irish Distillers LTD. In the middle of the 20th century, Irish whiskey almost completely disappeared from the world market. This one company stood alone, representing every bottle that said Irish whiskey. In the late 1960s, things changed when they bottled Jameson as a standalone brand. Think of how they market Jameson——smooth, triple distilled, with whiskey spelled with an "e." Sure, it saved an industry, but it also sold people a limited view of what Irish whiskey was in the past and what it can be.

The rules for Irish whiskey were revised almost half a century ago with the Irish Whiskey Act of 1980. These rules state that in order to use the name "Irish whiskey" a spirit:

- Must be distilled in the Republic of Ireland or Northern Ireland from a mash of cereal grains, fermented with yeast and distilled below 94.8% ABV, while retaining the flavor and aroma of the original grain.
- Must be aged in wooden barrels of 700 liters or less within the Republic and/or Northern Ireland for no less than 3 years.
- To be considered a blended whiskey, it must contain two or more distillates that follow the other stated rules of Irish whiskey.
- Must be bottled at 40% alcohol by volume or more.
- The only additional additives allowed during proofing include caramel coloring and water.

Also be aware that if a bottle carries an age statement, the youngest whiskey in the bottle is the oldest age that can be on the label.

You may also see additional words beyond Irish whiskey on a bottle. Here are four styles of Irish whiskey that have their own individual rules on top of those listed above:

Pot Still Whiskey

Many call this the "Irish style," as it drove the popularity of Irish whiskey in the 19th century. What makes it unique is the use of unmalted barley in the mash bill. It requires a minimum of 30% malted barley, 30% unmalted barley and up to 5%

of other grains, and is distilled in pot stills. To be considered a single pot still it must come from a single distillery.

> **Side note:** *At the time of writing, these rules were being reviewed. Historic mash bills typically used higher levels of other grains, like oats and wheat, and today's distillers are looking to bring back that flexibility.*

Malt

This requires a mash bill made up of 100% malted barley, distilled in pot stills. To be a single malt, it must come from a single distillery.

Grain Whiskey

This cannot exceed 30% malted barley and uses other unmalted cereals distilled in column stills. To be considered a single-grain Irish whiskey, it must come from a single distillery.

Blended

This comprises two or more styles of malt, pot still, and grain whiskey.

While visiting Irish distilleries, you may encounter the spirit known as poitín or poteen. As you will learn soon, this spirit has roots in Irish whiskey, but because it is not an aged spirit, it is not Irish Whiskey. In addition, its mash bill can stretch beyond cereal grains, using sugar beet molasses, whey, and potatoes. And when maceration occurs, up to 10% of the spirit can incorporate berries, apples, and indigenous plants. Poitín can range from 40% to 90% ABV; many still make it illegally in Ireland. Its name comes from the Irish word *pota*, meaning "small pot."

Now that you know what is and isn't Irish whiskey, let's dive into the spirit's fascinating history.

A Brief History of Ireland and its Whiskey

Head to the distilleries of Ireland and Scotland and you will hear claims of which country invented whiskey, which makes it better, and strong opinions on how to spell it. As an American, it is fun to see this friendly rivalry from a third-party position. Both countries have interesting theories and arguments. It's time to get past myth and lore to learn the story of Irish whiskey.

Historians believe distilling most likely originated in Mesopotamia. From here, the story weaves through Alexandria in Egypt and finds its way to the School of Salerno on the Italian Peninsula and into Spain thanks to the Moors. A popular theory suggests that the Franciscan monks brought distilling to Ireland from Spain in the 13th century. But there is also a chance the Celtic monks, who traveled throughout central Europe and the Italian Peninsula, may have brought stills back to Ireland and Scotland even earlier.

Because of its medicinal uses and purified state, distilled spirits earned the name "the water of life." The Latin name "aqua vitae," was the most prevalent translation, but it also went by "eau-du-vie" in France, "aquavit" in Scandinavia, and "uisce beatha" in Ireland and Scotland. Originally distilled out of grapes and doctored with spices and aromatics, distillers shifted from grapes to grains as the spirit moved north, including the use of oats, rye, wheat, and barley.

The first Irish mention of aqua vitae is in the Red Book of Ossory in Kilkenny from 1324. However, the first mention of a grain-based aqua vitae comes from 1494 in the Scottish Exchequer Rolls, when King James IV ordered eight bols of malt from Friar John Cor at Lindores Abbey. Still, the lack of aging and use of aromatics make this a distant ancestor of today's whiskey.

THE BATTLES AND EVOLUTION OF IRISH WHISKEY

Over the centuries, the relationship between the English crown and the Irish has been a tumultuous one. It is hard to understate the impact it had on the development, growth, and demise of Irish whiskey.

Starting with the Norman invasion in the 12th century, England looked to increase its dominance over Ireland. Yet over time, the Normans began to integrate with the Gaelic Irish, adopting their customs and language. Slowly English power on the island would shrink to an area around Dublin known as the English Pale. When the Norman Fitzgeralds took up arms against King Henry VIII, he stripped them of their power and declared himself King of Ireland. During the reign of his successor, Mary Queen of Scots, parliament created Ireland's first licenses for the distillation of spirits. Yet the crown had little power to enforce the law beyond the Pale. Mary decided the way to subdue the Irish was to confiscate their lands and hand them over to Scottish and English settlers. Thus began the plantations of Ireland.

The next century was a bloody one, as the very soul of Ireland was at stake. Attempts by the Irish Gaelic lords to beat the plantation system failed and resulted in the Flight of the Earls in 1607. Into this void, the Crown set up a system of patents, or monopolies, over distillation. Lord Deputy Sir Arthur Chichester granted distilling rights to Sir Thomas Phillipps in an area known as the Rowte in County Antrim. Bushmills references this 1608 license as its implied origin, although several distilleries occupied this territory. In reality, the royal monopolies ended under Oliver Cromwell after the English Civil War and it was over a century before Bushmills first established itself as a company in 1784. Meanwhile, the battles between planted Protestants and Irish Catholics would rage on.

Once the monarchy returned, Charles II imposed an excise tax on the production of alcohol—four pence per proof gallon of spirits. Yet local magistrates, many of whom also served as landlords, ignored the tax because of their cash poor tenants' penchant for paying rents in uisce beatha. Others went underground, creating illegal poitín.

The fragile monarchy in England once again faced turmoil in 1685 when a Catholic king ascended the throne. Defeated on Irish soil at the Battle of the Boyne, the tension created by James II's brief reign led his successor William of Orange to clamp down, stripping Irish Catholics of their rights to hold positions of authority and land ownership.

The Ulster-Scots, in the north of Ireland, also felt the pressure as rents increased and, as Presbyterian dissenters to the Anglican church, they too lost positions of authority. This led to over a half-million people migrating to America in the 60 years prior to the American Revolution. Known today as the Scots-Irish, the Ulster-Scots brought with them their distilling traditions, making rye whiskey in Pennsylvania and Maryland before moving south into the mountains and then out to the frontiers. Many American moonshiners can trace their roots back to this wave of immigration.

Despite all the turmoil, modern whiskey took shape in the first half of the 18th century. The first known appearance of the word is in the *Book of Scottish Pasquils*: "Whiskie shall put our brains in a rage." An inauspicious beginning. For the next one hundred years, newspapers in England, Ireland, and America predominantly spelled the word whiskey, while Scotland mostly ignored the "e." By the middle of 1800s, England would join its northern neighbor in dropping the "e" while the Ulster region of Ireland would become split on the spelling. There would be more growing pains, but whiskey, as we know it, was emerging.

PARLIAMENT WHISKEY VS POITÍN

For many, 1757 is when Irish distilling officially became an industry for it was that year that saw the licensing of two historic distilleries. The Roe family purchased and licensed a small distillery on Thomas Street, Dublin, that within a century grew to produce over two million gallons a year. Meanwhile, the Brusna Distillery in Kilbeggan had two lives: thriving as Locke's Distillery, dying out, and then returning to operation as the Kilbeggan Distillery in the 1980s.

Despite this, illicit poitín continued to be a thorn in the government's side. To counter it, they banned private distilling and required still makers to only produce stills with a capacity of over 200 gallons. A backlash occurred and small towns gave up their licenses to go underground.

The missing tax revenue, mixed with the costs of an expensive war in America, became a point of contention with Britain's Prime Minister, Lord North. In 1779, he restructured the excise laws and taxed distillers based on how much a still could theoretically produce. To make a profit, distilleries ran their stills fast and frequently. Quality suffered, as did the reputation of this so-called "parliament whiskey." As a result, Poitín's reputation only grew, and the government soon started to levy heavy fines when unlicensed stills were discovered. This led to attacks on revenuers in a poitín war in northwest Ireland. When the crown placed a tax on malted barley in 1785, Irish distillers simply increased their use of unmalted barley to avoid the tax. This grain would be the key component of the Irish style known as old Irish pure pot still whiskey. It became a symbol of Irish defiance and a whiskey style that would make them famous the world over.

THE COFFEY STILL AND THE FAMINE

Ironically, the massive growth of the Irish whiskey industry started with an armed rebellion against what would become its largest customer. Spurred on by revolutions in America and France, an Irish republican named Theobald Wolfe Tone took up arms against British rule. The mission failed, leading to the Acts of Union that created the United Kingdom of Great Britain and Ireland. But while the independence movement failed, for whiskey distillers the annexation into Great Britain opened up free trade with the entire British Empire.

Yet, before Irish distillers could succeed, parliament whiskey would have to be improved. And this is when an unlikely hero emerged.

Gravely wounded during the poitín wars in Donegal, an excise man named Aeneas Coffey became a leading voice for tax reform. He helped in the development of the landmark Excise Act of 1823 that lowered taxes for both Irish and Scottish distillers. With legal distilling affordable on both sides of the Irish Sea, a whiskey boom ensued. In twelve years, Ireland went from 32 licensed distilleries to 93 and innovation took off. Showing their confidence in the industry, the Murphy brothers in east Cork installed the world's largest pot still at their Midleton Distillery, with an incredible capacity of 31,648 gallons.

As for Aeneas Coffey, he turned his attention to improving the efficiency of distillation. There had been several attempts to speed up the process by tying pot stills together, but these attempts had all failed. The most promising continuous still concept came from a Scottish distillery owner, Robert Stein. Aeneas took that design and resolved its flaws. The Haigs and Steins of Scotland embraced it, while Irish distillers seemed to have a love/hate relationship with it. Coffey would see his best market in the gin trade of London and Scotland. Still, by the end of the 19th century, over 70% of Irish whiskey came from a Coffey still and he kept his office open in Dublin—his 1830 Coffey still design is still in use worldwide today.

But the whiskey that made Ireland famous was old Irish pure pot still whiskey. Its distinctive creamy body, grain heavy flavor, and spicy finish stands out against its pure malt competition. In fact, it was so oily that distillers ran it through the still three times to smooth it out without sacrificing flavor. With names like Powers, Roe, and Jameson growing in stature, the industry looked primed for growth. But there was trouble ahead for the Emerald Isle.

In 1805, parliament enacted the Corn Laws to encourage use of Irish grain at the expense of cheaper grains like American corn. This enriched land owners but poverty ran rampant among the lower classes. Many took to abusing gin and cheap whiskey. This led to the powerful temperance campaign of a preacher from Cork named Father Mathew. His cure was to cut alcohol completely out of the picture—over a third of the population took his "total abstinence" pledge.

Then, in 1845, a terrible potato blight moved from continental Europe into Ireland. Since its introduction to the island in the late 16th century, the spud had become a primary source of nourishment. Mismanaged by parliament, the famine led to the death of over a million people and the migration of a million more.

For the Irish whiskey industry, the combination of death, migration, and temperance cut the number of the country's distilleries in half.

THE GOLDEN AGE OF OLD IRISH PURE POT STILL WHISKEY

By 1860, a law change saw the rise of bonders and blending houses as the Gladstone government legalized the blending of malt and grain whiskey. In Scotland, the dynasties of malt and grain blenders like Johnnie Walker, Dewar's, and Buchanan's began. Irish distillers used the law to employ bonders as agents for selling their whiskey and distillers got out of the branding business.

With fewer Irish consumers, unsold stocks of old Irish pure pot still whiskey increased. It was around this time that a North American aphid started gnawing away at European vineyards. Brandy became scarce and Irish distillers took advantage by exporting their excess whiskey to fill the void. The quality of the spirit started paying dividends, as by the 1870s, London's W.A. Gilbeys saw Irish whiskey outselling scotch two to one.

But that golden reputation came at a cost as counterfeit Irish whiskey found its way into the market. It wasn't beyond some bonders to ship whiskey to Belfast, blend it, and then ship it out as genuine Irish whiskey. In 1878, Dublin's "Big Four" distillers—John Jameson, William Jameson, George Roe, and John Powers—had seen enough and released a book called *Truth's About Whisky*. In it, their target became the cheaper grain neutral spirits produced in column stills, something they referred to as "silent spirit," saying it wasn't whiskey at all.

John Powers & Sons went one step further, bottling small amounts of their whiskey with a gold label. Bottling was an expensive proposition in the 1880s, as fully automatic bottle lines were still years down the road. But the distillery wanted consumers to have a reference bottle so they could tell if the bonders were selling the genuine article or not.

A LONG PAINFUL FADE

So, how did such a highly respected Irish whiskey industry disappear into obscurity? Those looking for simple answers blame failing to adopt Aeneas Coffey's mass production patent still and lost revenue during American Prohibition. Yet the troubles that slowly smothered the Irish whiskey industry went well beyond and were anything but simple.

First, Irish distillers leaned a little too long on barrels and bonders. Jameson, for example, didn't bottle a whiskey with their name on it until after the industry completely collapsed. Powers showed their interest in quality with their gold label bottling, but a lack of conviction by not taking over full quality control. And by shipping barrels in an era rife with adulteration, they left their reputations in the hands of unscrupulous bonders. Meanwhile, their American counterparts pushed their government to pass the Bottled-in-Bond Act in 1897, giving distillers a way to prove the purity of their product.

Then trouble came from Scotland. A scotch whisky boom in the 1890s led to overproduction and mass speculation. The worst offenders were the Pattison brothers, who began buying up their own whisky to prop up its price. When the great bubble burst, shockwaves rippled across the whiskey world, demand plummeted, and over-leveraged distillers saw their businesses collapse.

The Scottish grain-whiskey firm Distillers Company LTD (DCL) stepped in and began buying up Scottish and Irish distilleries simply to shut them down. A group of northern Irish distilleries merged to compete with the DCL, but within two decades the Scottish giant would absorb them, too. The DCL scored another win when, in 1909, a Royal Commission noted how blended whiskey was outselling pot still and malt, confirming "silent spirit" was not only whisky, but the most popular kind.

As war broke out in Europe, the temperance movement had found its champion in British Prime Minister David Lloyd George. Suggesting that alcohol was doing more damage to the army than the Germans, he pushed parliament for total prohibition. When rebuffed, he settled for a lowering of minimum proof standards, worked to get cheap whiskey off the market by setting the minimum three-year age requirement for whiskey, and shut down distillery production during the war to, in his words, preserve grain for food.

Then Ireland faced its own crisis, as the Easter Rising in Dublin set off another independence movement. Rebels used distilleries as staging points while they awaited attacks from British reinforcements. A full scale War of Independence erupted in 1919, resulting in the country's partitioning into the Irish Free State and Northern Ireland. This only inflamed tensions, leading to the bloody Irish Civil War.

The combination of struggles at home, losing the American market to Prohibition, and conflicts with the British Empire exacerbated the problem. It also didn't help that American bootleggers like Al Capone were pawning off rot gut and calling it Irish whiskey.

To save old Irish pure pot still, the minimum age of whiskey in the Free State moved up to five years. By this time, however, blended whiskies from Scotland dominated the market and Irish tastes were moving to beer. Hoping to find greater profits at home, the Irish government put restrictions on whiskey exports, further exacerbating the problem. Distillery after distillery collapsed as Irish whiskey's price fell through the floor. As if the industry hadn't suffered enough, with only five distilleries remaining in the Free State, the government went into a trade war with their largest market—the British Empire.

By 1932, William Ross of the Scottish DCL referred to Irish whiskey as "irrelevant." The industry was so weak that when the American market opened back up after the repeal of Prohibition they were in no position to take advantage. Meanwhile, President Roosevelt's son James and his partner Joe Kennedy had stocks of scotch sitting off the coastline of New York, ready to feed the thirst of the American market. Northern Ireland and the new Irish Republic (as the Irish Free State became) missed their chance and Irish whiskey would be all but forgotten by 1960.

THE IRISH WHISKEY REVIVAL

The turnaround in Irish whiskey came out of capitulation. Seeing the writing on the wall, the three remaining family-owned distilleries in the Republic—John Power & Son, John Jameson & Son, and Cork Distilleries Company—merged to become Irish Distillers, LTD (IDL). They hired an outsider named Kevin McCourt who saw the potential of a united company. IDL made plans to shut down each of the individual distilleries and move the entire operation to a new distillery in Midleton, east Cork.

The only holdout was Bushmills in Northern Ireland as their parent company didn't want to sell to the IDL. Overseas, the Canadian company Seagrams liked what IDL was doing and made an offer to buy them. IDL used the opportunity to get what they wanted. If Seagrams bought Bushmills, IDL would offer 15% of the company in trade for the northern holdout. The ruse worked, and by 1978 the whole of Irish whiskey was under one umbrella, with two distilleries on the entire island.

With a monopoly over the industry, the IDL stopped the age-old practice of selling whiskey through bonders and released Jameson whiskey as its own independent brand. But their hopes that Seagrams would rapidly open new markets faltered. After several hostile takeover bids, IDL sold to the French-owned conglomerate Pernod Ricard.

The only thing that kept Irish whiskey from being 100% under French control was the purchase of the multi-use Cooley Distillery by lifelong entrepreneur John Teeling. He also purchased the historic Locke's Distillery in Kilbeggan and set about distilling and brand building. He kept the company churning along for 25 years, fighting off advances by his larger competitor and struggling with finances.

Meanwhile, IDL's new ownership put money behind promoting the Jameson brand. Sales grew from a mere 46,000 cases in 1988 to 4 million cases in 2012. Once again, Irish whiskey was available all over the world.

This success and the public's increasing interest in whiskey created a stir in the minds of Irish entrepreneurs. Distillery projects grow at Dingle, Echlinville, and West Cork. When John Teeling eventually sold Cooley to Beam Global in 2012, his sons Jack and Stephen Teeling left Cooley to build Dublin's first new distillery in over 125 years under the Teeling family name.

Since then, more and more entrepreneurs have joined the ranks of distillery owners as Irish whiskey heads toward a second golden age. Over the last decade, distilleries have started to dot the landscape from Cork to Belfast, Donegal to Waterford. Some have opened their doors, selling gin while their new make ages. Others have leaned on West Cork, Cooley, and John Teeling's Great Northern Distillery for sourced whiskey. And a few have reached into their Irish roots and brought back poitín. Over the next few years, as the results of their own distilling populates shelves, the grand return of old Irish pure pot still whiskey as single pot still whiskey will be complete. An industry that prided itself on quality and then collapsed into a single company will once again show the incredible ingenuity and diversity of Irish distilling.

HOW TO DIG EVEN DEEPER INTO IRISH WHISKEY HISTORY

This is simply a taste of the incredible stories, myths, and legends that surround Irish whiskey. If you just can't get enough Irish whiskey history, check out Season 6 of the *Whiskey Lore Stories* podcast on Apple Podcasts, Spotify, or your favorite podcast app. Or just go to **whiskey-lore.com**, click on the "stories" link and listen online. You can learn the full story of how the "e" got into Irish whiskey, the origins of Irish coffee, and tales of the hero and villain Aeneas Coffey in Season 6 of the podcast. And to hear interviews with the distilleries who are creating this second golden era of Irish whiskey, check out my other podcast Whiskey Lore the Interviews. Listen to history come alive as you travel between distilleries or to help give you more inspiration for the distilleries you want to visit.

Whiskey Production in a Nutshell

After visiting my first twenty distilleries, people would ask, "aren't you sick of hearing about the distillation process?" In a word, no.

The process is part of the reason each distillery visit is so unique. Hidden between the fermenters and pot stills are the little nuggets that separate one distillery or whiskey from another. Yes, the basic process is similar from one distillery to the next, but the equipment isn't the same; the fermentation times aren't the same; the grains used aren't the same; the warehouses aren't the same; the philosophies aren't the same, and so on.

This is where the book you are reading now is going to give you a leg up on the rest of your tour party. While they are trying to grasp the basics of whiskey production and distillation, you will absorb all the subtle nuances. And all that I talk about here will come alive before your eyes.

Don't worry, this isn't a chemistry lesson. I will keep to the basics and give you just enough information to enhance your experience. I'll also give you some suggestions of things to listen out for during your tour.

MALTING

After receiving grain from its source, a certain percentage is set aside for malting. This activates enzymes critical to the fermentation process. The grain typically used is barley. The maltster steeps it in water, drains it, and will typically lay it out on a malting floor. Enzymes turn starches into the sugars that hungry yeast will feed on.

When shoots appear, a kiln is used to stop growth and prevent the loss of sugars. If peat (or turf) is used in this process, it will impart a smoky character. Some distillery tours will allow you to smell and even taste malted and unmalted barley.

Even with modern techniques, malting is a labor- and time-intensive process and most distilleries have neither the space nor staff to do their own maltings. Malting houses like Minch Malt in Kildare will provide their own malted grain or will malt grain provided by the distilleries own farm source. But malting isn't just for barley. Keep your ears out for creative distillers that are using other types of malted grains like oats and rye.

MILLING

The next step in the process is to break down the grain by feeding it into a mill. I found various styles of mills throughout Ireland, including roller mills, hammer mills, and water-based hydro mills, or a combination of these. It's worth asking your tour guide what type of mill they use and why they chose that style.

Roller and hammer mills provide husks, flour, and grist. If so, some tour guides reveal a three-tier grist box to illustrate the process of separation. Some distilleries take these individual components and blend a unique ratio that works for them. The water-based hydro mill does not require separation and the results will look more like oatmeal.

GRAIN AND MASH BILLS

With the reemergence of old Irish pure pot still whiskey, now referred to as Pot Still or Single Pot Still style, the concept of grain or mash bills has once again entered the Irish whiskey vernacular.

> **Side note:** *Don't let the terms single malt, single grain, or single pot still fool you. The term "single" in each of these cases refers to creation at a single distillery, not the number of grains that are selected.*

Distilling of grain, or single grain whiskey, occurs in column stills, normally using less expensive grains like corn. However, some distilleries, like Royal Oak and Slane, distill barley and other grains. Regardless of the grain chosen, they include a small amount of malted barley to introduce enzymes into the grain bill.

Single malts can also have a unique mash bill. However, unlike its pot still and grain siblings, the grains must be a style of malted barley. Listen for single malt mash bills that contain different varieties of specialty malts like cherry wood smoked malts, chocolate malts, or Munich malts. There is also a move toward reviving heritage grains and organics.

At the time of writing, the official rules for pot still and single pot still whiskey are under review. The current regulations call for a minimum of 30% malted barley and 30% unmalted barley with only 5% maximum use of any other type of grain. However, distilleries like Blackwater, Killowen, and Boann, are using grain bills that date back to the early 1800s. These formulas use much less malted barley and generous amounts of unmalted barley, oats, wheat, and rye. This will be a fascinating development to watch play out as it expands our knowledge of legacy flavor profiles in Irish whiskey.

MASHING AND/OR LAUTERING

The next step in the process is to add the milled grain to water in either a mash tun, mash conversion vessel, and/or lauter tun; there are also combo units that do it all. During the cooking phase, they apply various temperatures depending on the grain; enzymes break down starch into sugars during this stage, creating a sweet liquid called wort.

Most distillers drain the wort through the false bottom of a lauter tun or combo unit. To extract maximum sugars, they add water to the spent grain, drain it, and add it to the wort mixture.

Waterford and Killarney Brewing and Distilling add a mash filter to the process. This is used to squeeze out the maximum amount of wort before distilling. The distillery collects the protein-rich spent grain and provides it to local farmers to feed livestock.

A few distilleries like Ardara do on-grain distilling. Here, the solids accompany the liquid into fermentation and even into the initial distillation.

FERMENTATION

The next step is to place the wort into a fermentation vessel called a washback. The distiller brings the temperature of the wort down to under 30°C or 90°F and adds dry or liquid yeast to the mixture. If the mixture is too warm, the yeast becomes lazy and if it gets too hot, it can kill them off. Yeast feeds on the sugars and releases both alcohol and CO_2.

The average fermentation time is around 72 hours, but distillers may allow the yeast to work longer to extract more fruity characteristics or less if deemed necessary. When the yeast is most active, it looks like the mixture is boiling, but this is simply the creation of CO_2.

Most washbacks have lids that stay shut during this process—if your guide opens the flap or door and lets you take a whiff, be careful! The CO_2 will take your breath away.

Distillers use either wooden or stainless-steel fermenters. Again, it is fun to ask the tour guide's opinion, is wood better than stainless steel? The variety of responses will surprise you.

DISTILLATION

Thanks to the yeast, we now have a fermented liquid akin to beer without the hops. Referred to as wash, it sits at 5 to 10% alcohol by volume. To raise the level of alcohol, the distiller uses a combination of stills. There are three primary types of stills used for the first distillation.

Pot Stills

Copper pot stills are traditional and produce spirits in batches. Some look like copper Hershey's Kisses or genie bottles, but they can also look very industrial. Pot stills are popular in Scotland and Ireland, and are ideal for making flavorful single malt and single pot still whiskeys. They are hollow vessels that use a heating source at their base to raise the temperature of the liquid. Some run on steam, some on gas power, and others, like Crolly and Killowen, still use the old flame to pot method. The alcohol vapors escape out of the top through a stem called a lyne arm. The direction and design of the lyne arm can increase copper contact, which cleans out unwanted sulfites.

One item you will see near the pot stills is a spirit safe. Governments once mandated these devices to keep distillers honest and tax revenue agents busy. Normally a copper and glass box, it contains bowls and moveable troughs where cuts are made in the spirit. This is where the skills of the distiller may have the greatest impact. A choice has to be made where to make heads (forshots), hearts, and tails (feints) cuts as the stills produce lower and lower concentrations of alcohol.

Heads are the high-alcohol spirits that come from the beginning of distillation (or run). This alcohol is mostly methanol and, if consumed, can make you sick and lead to blindness. During American Prohibition, rookie distillers or those with no conscience left this byproduct in their spirit—thus the stories of people going blind from drinking tainted hooch.

We call the middle of the run the hearts; this is the choice spirit that goes into barrels to age. Finding the beginning of the hearts run is critical, so even distillers using automation will manually control this step.

The tails are the leftovers after the hearts have run. Tails contain low proof alcohol that has a funky character. Distillers will discard them or re-distill them along with the heads in the next batch, to reduce waste.

With endless varieties of shapes, sizes, configurations, and the ability to choose wider cuts between heads, hearts, and tails, pot stills impart more influence on the flavor and body of a spirit than their more standardized cousin, the Coffey still.

Coffey (Patent) Stills

Continuously running Coffey column stills are popular with mass producers of grain whiskey like Midleton and Great Northern Distillery, but some smaller distilleries use them too. Distilleries like Slane and Royal Oak feel this gives them 100% control over the quality of their blends and single grain offerings.

You can identify the Coffey still by its height. The majority are two- to three-stories tall and set in pairs. Shaped like tall musical flutes, the first column, known as an analyzer, has a series of perforated plates that allow the wash to work its way down as steam through the bottom brings the liquid to a temperature between the boiling point of alcohol (78.37°C), and water (100°C). Alcohol vapor eventually escapes from the top of the still.

Next, concentrated alcohol flows into the bottom of the second column, called a rectifier, where it meets a series of bubble plates as the vapor rises; micro-distillations occur along the way. The distiller can then pick a specific proof level for the hearts. A Coffey still can produce alcohol that reaches right to the upper proof limits of Irish grain whiskey.

If space is an issue, they sometimes break column stills up into six pieces each, as with Slane Distillery and Great Northern Distillery. Here, the liquid rises and then has to drop to the next piece of the still, and so on until it reaches its final destination. Because many consider grain spirits to be neutral, smaller distilleries source their grain whiskey from larger distillers. In fact, even though Bushmills left Irish Distillers, LTD, they still source their grain whiskey from IDL's Midleton Distillery.

Side note: Don't confuse the Coffey still with the American bourbon-making beer still. Beer stills combine the analyzer and rectifier plates into a single column. From here, steam goes directly to a thumper, or the steam is condensed and sent to a doubler, for flash distillation. This setup allows the lower proofs required by bourbon regulations. As this book goes to press, there is at least one distillery in Ireland that has included a thumper in its setup, with the goal of making a sour mash whiskey.

Hybrid Stills

A hybrid still is just that, a combination of a pot still with a column still in the neck. These give distillers flexibility by adding the advantages of column-still distillation to pot-still distillation. However, hybrid stills are rare in Ireland.

EXTRA: TRIPLE DISTILLATION

Triple distillation simply means distilling through a pot still three times. If you see three pot stills at a distillery, it is a good bet they are triple distilling. However, I know of one distillery that uses the first or second still a second time to achieve triple distillation. There is another that just skips the third still when double distillation is required.

Does triple distillation create a smoother whiskey? Not necessarily. You can distill poor distillate three times and it still will still be poor distillate. Each distillation raises the percentage of alcohol, reducing the amount of harsh or funky congeners. But, the higher the ABV of the final product means less flavor from the distillate, leaving the barrel to do most of the work. If you really want to geek out, ask your tour guide if the distiller does heads and tails cuts off of both the second and third distillation—these cuts can affect the final ABV.

AGING

At this stage, the distiller has created a high-proof clear spirit called new make. However, as you will remember, the rules state that for something to be called Irish whiskey, it must live in a cask for three years.

Before being injected into the barrel, they may reduce the spirit proof using reverse-osmosis water. A hose is used to fill the barrel through the bunghole, and then the distiller hammers a bunghole stopper in, making the barrel ready for storage.

The choice of barrel is one of the most important parts of the process as these aging vessels will provide a substantial portion of the flavor and all the color of the spirit. Sherry and port casks are traditional but, because of their expense, are used primarily for a secondary maturation stage called finishing. Ex-bourbon barrels became cheap and plentiful after Prohibition, thanks to a law change that only allowed a barrel to be used once for bourbon production. Most Irish whiskey begins its maturation in an ex-bourbon barrel.

Each type of barrel has its own complexity and personality. Ex-bourbon barrels impart vanilla and toffee notes; Oloroso sherry butts provide dark fruit notes and a nutty character; Pedro-Ximénez (PX) sherry casks provide the sweetness of bright fruits; port pipes add a wine grape influence and hints of chocolate; virgin oak and reconditioned ex-bourbon barrels impart heavier vanilla, smoky char, and nutty oak influences.

But these are just the primary barrels used. One of Irish whiskey's significant advantages is its ability to be stored in barrels other than oak. Look for Irish whiskey aged or finished in chestnut, cherry, and acacia. This creates a whole new range of flavor profiles.

This brings us to my favorite part of the tour: the warehouse. Here you will experience the most pleasant smell of the entire tour. It is called the angel's share. And while it has a wonderful sounding name and scent, in reality it is the smell of whiskey being lost through evaporation. In Ireland, barrels lose around two percent of their contents to the angels, every year, with the first year being the most aggressive.

But more happens in the aging process than just evaporation. Changes in temperature between day and night and the seasons allow the wood of the barrels to expand and contract, soaking in and pushing out whiskey from the wood. In Kentucky, weather is more extreme, so aging happens faster—water evaporates more quickly than alcohol, so the ABV will rise with age. In the subtle weather of Ireland, wood interaction is less aggressive and aging happens over a longer period. With more humidity, alcohol evaporates faster than water, leading to the ABV dropping with age.

Traditionally, distilleries used a dunnage-style warehousing system where barrels lay on their sides on racks that stretched three to five levels high. These days, most Irish distillers have moved to palletised warehouses where the barrels stand head up on pallets that are stacked to the roof – this allows forklifts easy access, requires less physical labor, and improves safety.

How long should a whiskey age? Beyond the three-year requirement, there is no hard and fast rule. It all comes down to the skills of the blender and distiller. Older doesn't mean better. Aging is a tool that is used to reach a certain type of palate. Fans of smoky whiskey or whiskies with a lot of grain influence might prefer the new make's influence over that of the barrel. Fans of sherry-aged whiskeys may desire more barrel influence so they can find the barrel's personality in the whiskey. Older whiskeys can become complex with age, but they can also become one dimensional if aged in smaller barrels or for too long. This is the fun of tasting and discovering whiskeys: It gives you the opportunity to find the right combination that pleases you.

Sadly, not all distilleries age their whiskey on-site. Local officials usually frown upon a large warehouse filled with flammable liquid. And sometimes there just isn't enough room on the property for warehouses. Distilleries like Hinch use creative techniques to give you the warehouse experience without the need for an on-site warehouse.

Check out the profiles in this book or at whiskey-lore.com/distilleries and log in to see if a visit to the warehouse is part of the distillery's standard tour.

BOTTLING

When a whiskey has reached its desired age, the contents of the barrel are emptied into a trough through a mesh filter where the liquid is separated from unwanted particles and remnants of char. Very few distilleries show the area where this is done.

Some distillers employ a system of chill-filtering—dropping the whiskey's temperature below 0°C to assure the removal of any unwanted protein particles that may cloud the whiskey if they proof it below 46% ABV. The problem is, many feel this removes important oils and flavors from the whiskey. Today, there is a movement to remove chill-filtering from the process by increasing the ABV of whiskeys. Ask during your tasting if the distillery chill filters or look for whiskeys with "non-chill-filtered" clearly written on their labels.

Like scotch and most other world whiskeys, Irish whiskey allows the addition of a colorant additive called E150a. Some feel this caramel color makes the whiskey more attractive; others add it to create color consistency. Whether this additive changes a whiskey's flavor is up for debate.

The last step before bottling is the combining or vatting of barrel contents and proofing down. However, some Irish whiskeys go into the bottle at cask strength or come from a single barrel. To help you understand the journey of your whiskey, here are some terms you may encounter at the distillery or in your local whiskey shop:

Small Batch

There is no legal definition for how many barrels make up a small batch. So marketing departments use this term on anything from two barrels being married together up to thousands.

Single Barrel

This means the contents of the bottle came from a single barrel of whiskey. This can create some inconsistencies from bottle to bottle, but many people enjoy drinking one whiskey from a single source. Usually these whiskeys will have markings telling you the specific barrel it came from. It could also have a code telling you where it came from in the warehouse.

Cask Strength or Barrel Proof

This means no proofing took place during the bottling process. You are drinking exactly what came out of the barrel(s). Because the proof changes as a whiskey ages, many of these whiskeys will have the proof handwritten on the label.

Many large distilleries bottle off-site and out of view. Craft distilleries sometimes have the bottling done in the same room as the distillation process. Many distilleries use machines to bottle many of their whiskeys. At Tullamore D.E.W. and some other distilleries, there are opportunities for you to fill your own bottle, for an extra fee.

So have I got you champing at the bit to plan your Irish whiskey experience? Believe me, I have just given you a taste. If I sucked you in with the brief history of Ireland's whiskeys, then the profiles will help you find the distilleries that have a heavy focus on history. If the process fascinated you, then the profiles will point out distilleries that put an emphasis on the detail and science of distilling.

But before you jump too far ahead, it's time for me to give you the tools that will help you nail down the perfect plan for your dream trip to the Emerald Isle. Are you ready?

PART TWO

PLANNING YOUR ADVENTURE

~~~~~~~~

"Always carry a flagon of whisky in case of snakebite, and furthermore, always carry a small snake."

- **W.C. Fields**

PART 2
Planning Your Adventure

So many distilleries, so little time! Which one will you visit first? How many should you plan to tour? What is the best way to get around? Can you really plan this all out yourself, or should you hire a tour guide?

Personally, I love planning out adventures. As a traveler, my initials should be DIY. If you are the same, then this section will give you all the tools you need to plan your Irish whiskey experience. But maybe you would rather hire a tour guide to take the pressure off, or maybe you are on the fence about what to do. Whichever way you are leaning, this section should help you make educated decisions, so you get the most out of your travel time.

By the end of this chapter, you will:

- Understand the logistics involved in a do-it-yourself plan.
- Know the different strategies for conquering regions.
- Know how to pick the right mix of new and established distilleries.
- Have strategies for paring down your list to the perfect "must-see" distilleries.
- Know how many distilleries you can visit in a day.
- Know how to get around the island (safely) to the distilleries.
- Know how to plan accommodations.
- Be ready to use the profiles in the back of the book to plan your adventure.

As you reach the end of this chapter, I will have you armed with all the information you need to nail down your own personalized Irish whiskey experience, using the distillery profiles at the end of the book as your guide.

Travel Choices

On any whiskey adventure I take, an important consideration is always to avoid drinking and driving. Ireland and Northern Ireland have taken a hardline stance on this subject and so it is your responsibility to act within the parameters of the laws.

Because whiskey tourism is an emerging concept across the island, there isn't a uniformity in how the distilleries pour out samples or handle drivers. I expect this to evolve with time, as it did in Kentucky and Scotland. This means if you choose to drive, you will have to use your best judgment.

I almost hired a tour company on my first whiskey adventure just so I could sit back, relax, and enjoy the experience without worrying about how to get around. But in the end I took a chance, rolled on, and kept my schedule conservative. Later in this chapter, I will divulge some of my own experiences to help you understand strategies. That way you can hire a tour guide because you want to, rather than doing it through fear or uncertainty.

GOING BY TOUR GUIDE

There are many advantages to hiring a tour guide. Tour companies can be a great way to meet other whiskey enthusiasts and enjoy the day without having to put your hands on the wheel. Tour guides sometimes provide extra perks and experiences because they have established a special relationship with a distillery. They are experts that can provide additional commentary and history as you travel between destinations. And most tours provide a packaged lunch or special dining experience along the way.

Drawbacks to tour guides include less flexibility, a slower pace, and higher costs. If they offer multiple tour paths, you still need to know how to choose between the groups of distilleries in each package. So, if you plan to hire a tour guide, keep this book and its profiles handy to help you make informed decisions.

> *Side note: If you go with a guided tour, confirm whether the cost of the guide also includes the entry fee to the distilleries. This is not always the case.*

There are several tour companies that provide Irish whiskey experiences. Note that some may be regional. I have not used these companies myself, but they get good social media reviews. Do your own research by reviewing the comments left on TripAdvisor. com. If you are interested, ask about potentially customizing your tour.

Cellar Tours
cellartours.com/ireland/private-tours/whiskey

Whiskey Island Tours
whiskeyisland.ie

Butlers Tours
butlerstours.com/distillery-tour-ireland.php

DO-IT-YOURSELF

If you want flexibility, there is no better way to plan an Irish whiskey experience than to do-it-yourself. Planning your own trip allows you to choose the specific distilleries you want to visit, collect stamps in the Irish Whiskey 360° Distillery Passport, mix and match distilleries, take side trips, and experience Ireland at your own pace. But perhaps the best part of DIY planning is getting to cherry pick the distilleries that best fit your personality.

I have also experienced some pleasant surprises by planning my own adventures.

Because I like to travel in the morning and in the off-season, I have had many instances where I was the only one on the tour and, as a result, received VIP treatment. Or where the tour guide, on finding out that I already knew the whiskey-making process, focused the tour on additional behind-the-scenes information, going completely off script. I have also had opportunities to get extra tastes, talk directly to a distiller, and even enjoy whiskeys straight from the barrel.

The drawbacks to DIY include finding the time to plan, potential planning inexperience, transportation worries, and listening to the same old music or news in the car instead of a tour guide who will provide you with whiskey stories and anecdotes between stops.

That said, keep reading because we will solve the first three issues in the next few pages. And I can't recommend highly enough (though I might be extremely biased) that you replace the dusty old tunes and news with downloaded episodes of the *Whiskey Lore Stories* podcast to supplement your Irish whiskey knowledge. Season six is all about Irish whiskey and you will get previews of many of the distilleries included in this guide. Find it on Apple podcasts, Spotify, and your favorite podcast app.

Okay, enough with the personal plugs. Before I help you pick out your dream list of distilleries, here is an option to consider.

The Irish Whiskey 360° Distillery Passport

If you are like me, two or three distilleries just won't tame your appetite for Irish whiskey. Amaze your friends by collecting stamps at each distillery you visit with an Irish Whiskey 360° Distillery Passport. Available in the visitor's center of any participating distillery, this guidebook not only provides evidence of the distilleries you've visited, it also makes a fine keepsake.

At the beginning or conclusion of your tour, show a member of the staff your book and receive that distillery's stamp in your Distillery Passport. If you are forgetful like me, keep this booklet in the front seat of your rental car or easily accessible in your travel bag and then get the stamp when you first arrive. I have found that I often forget about it at the end of a tour and the guides don't always ask for your whiskey passport.

Keep in mind that the booklet is still new and not all the distilleries listed in it are open to the public yet and that the list will change and grow. Also, these are a list of participating distilleries—it is not a comprehensive list. Its sponsors, Drinks Ireland and the Irish Whiskey Association, do not provide guides or transportation. Ultimately, it is just another fun way to do-it-yourself.

Creative Ways to Choose Distillery Tours

One thing that I have learned about touring distilleries in Ireland and Northern Ireland is that there is a distillery for everyone. The challenge is finding the one that speaks to you.

The easiest way is to find the name of a distillery or brand you are familiar with and just go there. But what is the fun of trying something you already know? It is time to stretch yourself and use this opportunity to discover new favorites and enjoy new experiences. Whether you're into historic distilleries, chocolate and food pairings, sensory experiences, Irish history, ghost stories, crafted cocktails, or smelling the angel's share, you will find a distillery suited to what you love.

Here are some creative ways to curate your perfect list of distillery experiences.

OLDER DISTILLERIES VERSUS BRAND NEW

There is a major temptation to just go with well-established brands you are familiar with. There is nothing wrong with that. But if you are planning on visiting two or more distilleries, a mix of experiences will give you an appreciation for all that Irish distillers offer.

Established Distilleries

While the Irish whiskey rebirth means that almost all distilleries are relatively new, some are more established than others. For instance, Teeling, Pearse Lyons, and Dingle have been entertaining guests on tours for at least a decade. Bushmills, Midleton, and Kilbeggan stand as the old guard with significant histories and large corporate experience behind them, so their tours are well polished.

Other distilleries like Waterford, Echlinville, and West Cork are well-established members of the new guard, yet their tours are just being established or have limited access. This means their tours may be a little more unstructured, providing some of the grit you'll experience in newer distilleries.

The major advantage of visiting established distilleries is that you may be able to taste whiskeys that were produced on-site, unlike at many new distilleries where they start out aging sourced whiskey from third parties. That said, there are always exceptions to the rule. Some distilleries are waiting beyond the required three years to release their whiskey; Echlinville is a great example, but their sourced whiskey is incredible and well worth tasting, and you might just visit on the day they finally release their own spirits. Use the profiles in the back of the book to get an idea of when to add these distilleries to your itinerary.

If you are lucky enough to have room for a handful of distilleries on your trip, mixing in at least one of the old guard with one of the established new guard will give you a more diversified impression of this Irish whiskey rebirth.

New Distilleries

If you are taking this trip to see where Irish whiskey is going, the new distilling kids on the block will energize you almost immediately. They are really pushing the boundaries of what Irish whiskey can be; some of this innovation comes from Irish whiskey's forgotten past and some of it from pushing the boundaries of what whiskey is.

Just because a distillery is new doesn't mean it lacks history. There are several distilleries setting up shop in historic buildings. From a carpet and doll factory at the Crolly Distillery, to a mill house on the historic Powerscourt Estate property, and in the former horse stables at Slane Castle, these distilleries give you a peek into not only whiskey's past but also a people's past.

And, as you would expect, some of these distilleries are state-of-the-art, like Killarney Brewing and Distilling, Waterford, and Boann.

There are the smallest of small distilleries where the owners may interrupt their work to take you on the tour, like at Killowen and Baoileach. There are distilleries that focus on single malts, and others on single pot still and poitín. Some distilleries are using turf (peat) dried malt to make incredible smoky whiskeys, while others are focusing on aging in the finest of sherry and port casks.

Some of these new distilleries have aspirations of becoming larger distilleries, some want to be tourist destinations, others want to control every piece of the process to create a genuine sense of terroir, while others just love the creative outlet whiskey provides and take each day as it comes.

These newest distilleries are a great opportunity to walk the floor, maybe meet the distiller, taste the new make, or draw whiskey straight from the barrel.

But don't focus too much on the distillery's age. As you will find, there are many other considerations that will take precedent. But once you have a list nailed down, make sure you have at least one old-school and one new distillery in your final plans. This will keep you from getting a limited view of Irish whiskey.

CONQUERING A REGION

Ireland is not an island of distilleries you can conquer in a week, so when planning a trip you will need to think about how far you want to go—and for how long. Traveling all around the island might force you to be in the car more than you want to be.

I would recommend instead picking a region and spending a day or two enjoying the best the area has to offer. In this guide, I have split Ireland and Northern Ireland into five separate regions that are manageable enough for you to be able to schedule at least two tours per day.

Here are the regions I cover in the distillery profiles:

Dublin

The capital of the Republic of Ireland and the largest city on the island, Dublin provides a variety of entertaining and scenic attractions. The distilleries here are easily accessible by foot, but a daily or three-day bus pass can help with more aggressive itineraries. It is easy to spend three days in town and not run out of distilleries, pubs, and museums to visit. Dublin also works well as a bookend to longer trips. The local currency is the Euro (€).

Midlands

Most people head to the city centers or the coasts when planning trips to Ireland, but you miss so much of the heartbeat of the country by doing that. A trip to the ancient east and heartlands will take you back in time, as they're home to the oldest distillery and oldest pub in Ireland. You'll also see castles, ancient ruins, lush green rolling hills, and have plenty of opportunities for recreational experiences. The local currency is the Euro (€).

Northern Ireland

When driving north, other than the switch from kilometers to miles, you may hardly notice that you have changed countries. But head to your first distillery and you will suddenly experience a different vibe. Belfast makes a great base of operations, as you can take day trips out to the distilleries of the Ard Peninsula or up to Bushmills and the Giant's Causeway. At night you can enjoy the benefits of the city with fantastic food and historic pubs, and there will soon be two new distilleries. The local currency is the Pound (£).

North Wild Atlantic Way

The Wild Atlantic Way features some of the most beautiful and iconic locations in Ireland. The northern regions exude Ireland's rebellious spirit, and the distilleries of this area reflect that. Here you will find the greatest diversity of spirits on the island—from smoky to sweet, from pot still to poitín. The local currency is the Euro (€).

South

This is where the influence of the sea meets the creative spirit of Ireland's distillers. You will need more than a couple of days to visit the great distilleries of southern Ireland, but it is time well spent. The region is home to the largest pot still in the world, as well as a focus on terroir, grain-to-glass distilleries, and an embracing of the sea. I have included the southern part of the Wild Atlantic Way in this region. The local currency is the Euro (€).

CREATING YOUR SHORT LIST OF DISTILLERIES

With the considerations of the region and distillery types in the back of your mind, it is time to start sketching out a list of tours you want to take.

Normally, this would be a daunting task and most people would default to looking up distillery names that are familiar. But I am about to empower you with a more personalized and logical way of picking your list.

Let me start by saying that you don't need to be overwhelmed by all the information this guide provides on each of the included distilleries. I'm going to give you some creative ways to approach these profiles, so you can quickly and easily gather an optimal list of places to visit.

Once you achieve that list, you can then organize the distilleries by region and begin planning out your days. My suggestion is to choose the best two or three pruning methods from the following list, then jot down the five region names on a piece of paper, leaving a space underneath, and adding each distillery you choose to its corresponding region. Jot down the primary reason you want to visit as it might help you narrow things down later.

If you are like a kid in a candy store and your list looks long, it's okay. I tend to choose up to three times more distilleries than I intend to visit. This way I can whittle my list down to the best of the best or to the ones that best fit my schedule.

Here are my favorite pruning methods for creating a short list of distilleries. Choose your list by:

Distilleries You Know

Sure, this is the basic method that most people use, but it is common for a reason. You don't want to miss a distillery you've been looking forward to seeing your whole life. Look through the list of distilleries and add the ones you are most curious about.

Brands You Know

This is the most logical way to choose a distillery, but sometimes it's difficult to know who makes which brand.

Never fear: I have included a handy brand guide in the back of this book. Scribble down your favorite brands, then find them in the alphabetical list and write down each brand's corresponding distillery. For example, if you like The Dubliner, on the list you will see it comes from the Dublin Liberties Distillery in the Dublin region. If you like Redbreast, it matches up with the Old Midleton Distillery in the South region. And if you are curious about Dunville's, Echlinville Distillery in the Northern Ireland region is where the guide directs you. When you compile your list, write the brand name with the distillery name, so you don't forget the connection.

But remember, just because that distillery makes a particular whiskey doesn't mean you will get to sample it at the end of your tour.

To help you get a sense of what you might taste during your visit, I have included mentions of some whiskeys that might be available to experience in each distillery profile. Use this as a loose guide to help you get an idea of what you might be tasting.

However, remember that tasting selections can change without notice. The purpose of these tastings is for the distillery to entice you to buy what they want to sell. So it's most likely that your offerings will be popular whiskeys or something new they want you to add to your collection. Don't expect a sample of Redbreast 27-year-old whiskey at Old Midleton. That said, I have encountered some unexpected surprises during my tastings at some distilleries, so enjoy the surprise when it happens.

Recommendations

When I started planning my first distillery adventure, I found traveler reviews on Google Maps and TripAdvisor helpful in providing further confirmation of my choices. I will warn you though, most people love just about every distillery tour they go on, and many reviewers have only experienced one or two distilleries. So try to dig beyond the overall accolades and see if you can spot something specific that might draw you to that distillery. Also remember that distilleries may have multiple tour guides with different experience levels, stories, and personalities. So don't expect to have the same guide or experience as the reviewer.

Friends and acquaintances can also be a great resource for advice. Maybe you have a friend who has recently returned from a trip around Ireland, in which case see what distilleries they enjoyed. If you are at your favorite pub or at a whiskey festival, ask bartenders or patrons for their advice on distilleries they have visited.

Social media can also provide a wealth of feedback. Instagram, Facebook, YouTube, and Pinterest feature thousands of people who have traveled to distilleries and who would love to recommend their favorites.

One of the most overlooked sources for great distillery advice is from other tour participants. While you are enjoying a tour, talk to others about their favorite distillery visits. This can be helpful in planning your next trip or filling in gaps in your current itinerary. And that leads me to another piece of advice: If you are in a region for two days or more, plan in flex time. It never fails that someone will mention another tour in such glowing terms you will kick yourself for not having enough extra time to visit.

Enhanced Experiences

I have loaded the profiles in this book with information on standard distillery tours, but most distilleries also offer enhanced experiences such as deeper tastings or extended tours.

For example, I love whiskey, and I love food pairings. While traveling, I learned that Powerscourt Distillery has an in-house food historian who guides visitors through a pairing of local foods and the distillery's Fercullen whiskey on weekends. This guided tasting and tour provided an excellent enhancement to the history and distilling lessons of the standard tour.

Also, keep your eye out for special events. Distilleries like Crolly, Burren, and Echlinville are looking to provide deeper educational or hands-on experiences. And several distilleries provide unique holiday themed tours, behind-the-scenes tours, or even the chance to see the distillery without a formal tour.

If you want to immerse yourself in a particular distillery, there may be a possibility of doing extended tastings at the end of the tour—or you might skip the tour all together and just do the tasting. Some distilleries have their own pubs and cocktail lounges available at the end of the tour. Just make sure you have a designated driver or use a local taxi service if you are planning an extra taste.

If you are visiting five or more distilleries on a trip, I highly recommend choosing some kind of special experience for at least one of your distillery visits. Variety is the spice of life, and it adds zest and depth to any distillery experience.

Price

Unfortunately, tours cost money and your decision on which distilleries and how many you visit could come down strictly to budget. And, like everything else, tour prices have gone up and may fluctuate, which makes planning even tougher.

I wanted to place exact pricing for tours in the distillery guide, but by the time this reaches you, the prices could have changed. So I have added in currency symbols to show you a range of prices.

In the Republic of Ireland, here's what each symbol relates to:

- Free   = Free
- €   = €0.01–12
- €€   = €13–24
- €€€   = €25–36
- €€€€   = over €37

In Northern Ireland, here's what each symbol relates to:

- Free   = Free
- £   = £0.01–10
- ££   = £11–20
- £££   = £21–30
- ££££   = over £31

Use these figures as an estimate, then double check the current prices on the distillery's website before making your final decision. Don't forget to make reservations for the most important tours, especially if you are traveling during a busy tourist season or the distillery mandates it. Tours do frequently sell out. And know that extended tastings and special experiences will cost more.

Distillery History and Architecture

Ireland is full of amazing history and architecture. Where do you begin? And with an industry just returning from a long slumber, it's easy to expect that historic distilleries would be hard to find, but sites like Midleton and Kilbeggan will take you back into the boom years of the 19th century.

Some distilleries focus on their regional distilling traditions, like Micil and Lough Ree on the North Atlantic Way and Dublin Liberties in Dublin. Other distilleries focus on the rich history of their area, such as Powerscourt and Clonakilty. For the history buff, the choices are endless.

With architecture, some distilleries are preserving history by building their distilleries in historic structures, like the Ahascragh Distillery that occupies a historic mill and Waterford in an old brewing house. And while you're visiting the beautiful medieval churches in Dublin, check out the church that was transformed into Pearse Lyons Distillery.

Location and Region

Are you heading to Ireland to explore your family roots? Been wanting to kiss the Blarney Stone? Or maybe your long-lost aunt lives in Cork. With distilleries all over Ireland, you are likely to have a distillery near where you are visiting.

Perhaps you have already visited a couple of distilleries in one area and want to experience another region of Ireland. Donegal is just a short flight away from Dublin, or head to the foodie town of Kinsale and enjoy some great distilleries along the way. If you make that first trip to Belfast, you'll get to see the rejuvenation of Northern Ireland first hand.

One of the best regions for a first-timer is Dublin. Get a hotel or an Airbnb; stroll around the historic Liberties and enjoy distilleries, amazing food, whiskey bars, pubs, nighttime entertainment, and the Bow Street Jameson Museum. And as an Irish whiskey fan, you should definitely make time to visit the Irish Whiskey Museum. Your guide will take you on a fun journey through the history of Irish whiskey. You will see the historic brands of Irish whiskey through time, and finish with some great whiskey samples.

KEEP A WISH LIST

It will be hard to see every Irish whiskey distillery you want to see during a single trip. Keep a list from your current research or bookmark the distilleries that will require a future visit. By using the online distillery guide and wish list feature at whiskey-lore. com/distilleries you can make sure you don't lose track of your selections. As you try new whiskeys or talk to friends about your trip, your list is going to grow. A wish list will help you be prepared for planning your next Irish whiskey experience.

If you just can't stand it anymore, take some time to view the distilleries in the back of this book and start making your top ten or 20 list right now. When you feel you have the ultimate list of distilleries picked out, come back to this section and I will help you figure out how to arrange them, schedule time for them, secure your tour reservations, and plan your lodging and transportation.

The Logistics of Distillery Planning

This is where it gets very real! You have committed to the trip. You have decided on all the distilleries you would like to visit. Now it's time to create your itinerary.

HOW MANY DISTILLERIES PER DAY?

How many distilleries can you plan to visit in a single day? Well, that depends on how intense you or your companions want to be. It also depends on the tours you are doing, the region you are visiting, and the day of the week. On a normal day, it is possible to do three standard distillery tours. It would be possible to plan four tours, if they are all in a very centralized area like the Dublin Liberties and one of them stays open past 5 p.m., but it will put you in a rush. Remember to build in time for meals and diversions, as well as flex time, so you have the option to add another distillery on the fly.

If you are traveling with others, remember that not everyone may want to tick off distilleries as quickly as you. If that is a potential concern, make sure you leave even more flex time in your schedule.

If you plan some extended tours or tastings, schedule those for the end of the day. It is hard to determine how much longer these events will run and most likely you will want to linger after the allotted time to chat with fellow travelers and enjoy an additional dram or cocktail.

If you are heading out west and south, it will be difficult to fit in three or more distilleries in a single day. Keep in mind the amount of driving time between each distillery.

The day of the week will also matter. Not all distilleries are open seven days a week. The most usual days off are Monday or Tuesday, but some places only conduct tours on the weekends. This will increase the possibility of not being able to reach as many distilleries in a day as you might like. On Sundays, it is pretty standard for distilleries to start their tours at noon or later, which will likely prevent you from reaching three distilleries in a day.

In the distillery profiles, I provide the days of the week the distillery is open to help you get your basic plans down. In future editions, I will add the times for the tours as well. At the time of writing, distilleries are still solidifying their hours, so you will need to check the websites when nailing down your exact schedule. Remember, it is always good to make reservations once you lock in your plans.

HOW MUCH TIME TO PLAN FOR EACH DISTILLERY?

It is very easy to over-schedule your day when planning distillery visits, and a loaded schedule can cause stress and frustration. Let's look at some factors you should consider when spacing out your distillery visits on your itinerary.

The first factor is tour length. When you look at the distillery profiles, you'll notice I haven't listed how long the tours are. This is because tour times can vary drastically.

Here is basically what you can expect: if a tour is 60 minutes long, this usually means the first 45 minutes will be the actual tour and the last 15 minutes will be the tasting—but not always. I have been on some tours that run for 60 minutes before the tasting. Make sure you get an idea of the tour length when making your reservation, as many distilleries will list this in the description.

Sometimes, outside factors extend the time needed to visit a distillery. If a tour guide is talkative or if guests ask a million questions, then you are heading for added time. Or you may hit it off with fellow travelers and want to continue a fun conversation, but the pinch of a tight itinerary has you running away.

I would recommend that you pad your distillery time with an extra 30 minutes, at the very least.

The next factor is a transportation delay. Never assume you will get to the next location without hitting every stop light, getting distracted by an unscheduled stop off, having a bus or train delayed, or being slowed by a traffic incident. Plan your time out, but add 15 minutes or more to give yourself a cushion for unexpected travel events.

We all have to eat and it is even more important to keep our bellies content on a day filled with whiskey samples. Build in a lunch break of an hour or more—and a dinner hour if you're planning an early evening tour.

The last factor you should keep in mind is that distilleries like you to check in for your tour 15 minutes ahead of its starting time. Don't push things until the last minute or you might lose your chance to tour—or, worse still, you might hold up the other visitors.

SHOULD YOU MAKE RESERVATIONS?

Irish distillery tours will continue to get more and more popular as more people discover them. As a result, it has become much more important to consider making reservations, especially during the busy summer season or if you are doing a limited-edition tour.

The simplest way to get tickets is to use the distillery's website to do so, ideally as soon as you know your plans. Don't worry, there shouldn't be anything to print: I have never had a distillery host ask me for a printed ticket (just make sure you have access to your email in case they lose your reservation). In most cases, the distillery will just verify your reservation by name when you arrive. Another option is that if you will be in an area for two or more days, stop by the distillery the day before you want to visit and attempt to secure your tickets in person.

Just be aware that there are exceptions to every rule. Some distilleries stop taking reservations online two days before the tour starts. You may get walk-up tickets, but you might also miss out.

To save you from hunting around websites, I provide a more information link for each distillery within their profile. Here, you can log in and directly access the distillery's tour reservation page.

ARE CHILDREN ALLOWED ON TOURS?

While distilleries welcome children in the visitor's center and gift shop, many impose an age restriction for the tour itself. I have heard this described as being for health and safety, insurance, or legal reasons. Children under eight are typically excluded, but check with the distillery to make sure. They sometimes offer older children discounts for tours and provide non-alcoholic drink choices. If you are planning to take children under ten years of age on your distillery journey, you will save a lot of headaches by reaching out to the distillery to confirm before you plan a visit with a child.

Getting to and Around Ireland

Once you have your rough sketch of distilleries completed, it is time to figure out how to traverse the island. Planes, trains, buses, and automobiles are at your disposal.

And what about the concern about drinking and driving? Yes, I will cover that too.

BY PLANE

If you don't live on the Emerald Isle, your best bet for reaching Ireland and Northern Ireland is to hop aboard a jet. There are three primary airports that provide easy access to various regions.

Dublin Airport (DUB)

Located north of the city of Dublin, this is the most popular option for flying into Ireland. From here you can take one of several buses that travel between the airport and the heart of the city or pick up a reserved car hire at the rental agency.

If you only need a bus to take you in and out of the city, the Dublin Express (dublinexpress.ie) is your fastest way into town. Purchase tickets in advance online. The pickup point is just below the walkway between the car-rental agencies and Terminal 2.

The best option for longer stays or easier travel within the city is with Dublin Bus (dublinbus.ie). Consider buying a three-day pass if you're in the city for a few days; this allows you to ride the local buses and trains. Tickets can be purchased in advance online or you can buy your ticket at the Spar store on the second floor in Terminal 2. At the airport, the bus pickup point is a short walk beyond the Dublin Express stop. Look for Zone 15 and the yellow bus. Once you board the bus, hold your ticket on the scanner until you hear a single beep. If you pull off too fast, it will beep twice, which signifies it didn't catch your scan. Once you reach the center of town, you will be near four distilleries. Those driving rental cars will have easy access to distilleries in the Midlands from this airport. The local currency is the Euro (€).

Belfast International Airport (BFS)

Located a fair distance west of the city, Northern Ireland's biggest airport is ideal for car rentals but requires a little more effort if you need bus transportation into the city. The best option is to take the Airport Express 300 bus; tickets can be purchased in advance online (translink.co.uk) or via the mLink app on your mobile device. Once in the city, a daily Translink pass provides easy access to all of Belfast; ticket purchasing kiosks are conveniently placed at multiple train and bus stops.

Belfast airport is ideally placed for the Northern Ireland distilleries; because many of the distilleries are rural, I recommend renting a car. (Though be aware that Belfast will soon have two new distilleries.) The local currency is the Pound (£).

Shannon Airport (SNN)

If you are planning to spend most of your time around the towns of Galway, Limerick, Cork, or Killarney, Shannon Airport may be your best option. Car hires will get you to any of these destinations in less than two hours and will be the easiest way to reach rural distilleries. The national bus service Bus Éireann is also an option (find the link in the section "By Bus"), but local transportation will be required to reach most distilleries. This is the ideal airport for distilleries in the South region. The local currency is the Euro (€).

Other regional and city airports include:

George Best Belfast City Airport (BHD)

If you are flying in from Europe or within the United Kingdom, this airport could be a viable option. Its proximity to Belfast makes bus transportation into the city much faster. A variety of discount airlines, as well as KLM and British Airways, service this airport. I still recommend renting a car from here as, at the time of writing, all distilleries are currently rural—though Titanic and McConnell's are coming soon to Belfast. Use the Airport Express 600 bus provided by Translink. This airport easily serves the Northern Ireland region. The local currency is the Pound (£).

Cork Airport (ORK)

Another option for the South region, this regional airport will require a rental car for your onward journey as this area distilleries are rural. Bus Éireann and TFI Local Link bus transportation are available. The local currency is the Euro (€).

Derry Airport (LDY)

This regional airport isn't close to any current distilleries but could be a jumping-off point for car rental drivers exploring the North Wild Atlantic Way region. However, this may add to the logistics, as your trip west into Donegal will have you exchanging currency almost immediately. The local currency in Northern Ireland is the Pound (£) but Donegal is in the Republic of Ireland and uses the Euro (€).

Donegal Airport (CFN)

This airport easily serves the West region. As it's a regional airport, expect a higher price for your plane ticket and the need for a car hire to reach your destination. The local currency is the Euro (€).

Kerry Airport (KIR)

Another option for the West region, this regional airport will most likely require a rental car for your onward journey. The local currency is the Euro (€).

Waterford Airport (WAT)

This airport is an option for visiting the South region. There is a distillery in Waterford and new distilleries opening within a 90-minute drive by rental car. The local currency is the Euro (€).

BY TRAIN

This may not seem like the modern way to travel, but a train can be a unique way to enjoy a nice comfortable seat while letting somebody else take you to your destination. Visit Ireland's distilleries the way Alfred Barnard did back in the 19th century, but with a little more luxury.

Be aware that trains will only get you close to your distillery destinations, and alternate transportation may be required:

Iarnród Éireann (Republic of Ireland)

Irishrail.ie
Irish Rail has two lines that serve the Republic:

Dublin Heuston

From Dublin's Heuston Station (a 20 minute walk from center city) serving Cork, Tralee, Limerick, Galway, Westport, Ballina and Waterford.

Dublin Connolly

From Dublin's Connolly Station (a 5 minute walk from center city) serving Sligo, Wexford, Rosslare Europoort and Belfast.

TransLink (Northern Ireland)

Translink.co.uk
The NI Railway lines head from Belfast to Derry, Bangor/Portadown, and Larne Line.

The Enterprise

Travel between Dublin's Connolly Station and Belfast's Lanyon Place. Book using TransLink in Belfast or Iarnród Éireann in the Republic. Purchasing roundtrip tickets is suggested, to avoid having to purchase on both sites.

BY BOAT

Feeling adventurous? There are ways to get to Ireland by boat. Be aware that boat travel can be seasonal.

Irish Ferries

Irishferries.com
Holyhead (Wales) to Dublin, Pembroke (Wales) to Rosslare, or Cherbourg (France) to Dublin.

Stena Line

Stenaline.co.uk
Liverpool (England) to Belfast.

BY BUS

National and local bus systems can provide transportation between cities, towns, and villages, and are an option if you want to leave the driving to others. Some distilleries are along these paths, making access easy, but many rural distilleries will require extra transportation options like taxis or some walking to get you to your destination. Check the websites for bus service to determine whether one of these easily serves your distillery.

Bus Éireann (Republic of Ireland)

buseireann.ie
A bus line for regional travel throughout Ireland, plus city bus services in places like Limerick, Cork, and Galway.

TFI Local Link (Republic of Ireland)

transportforireland.ie/tfi-local-link
Need a shuttle bus between towns and villages? Local Link comprises 15 different regions throughout the Republic that interconnect area communities.

Expressway (Republic of Ireland)

expressway.ie
A quicker way to get between larger destinations.

Dublin Bus (Republic of Ireland)

dublinbus.ie
Bus and train services around the city of Dublin and to the airport.

Translink (Northern Ireland)

translink.co.uk
Bus services in Belfast and across the country via Ulster Bus (part of Translink). Also available through Translink is Goldline, an express service between larger destinations in Northern Ireland.

BY RENTAL CAR

Love a road trip? Ireland is an incredible place to explore. It's a land of castles, incredible landscape features, and hundreds of picturesque towns and villages. A car gives you the ultimate way to access this marvelous island.

A car will provide you with total freedom, not least because very few distilleries are within walking distance of other distilleries, accommodations, or public transportation.

If you have a partner or are traveling in a group, it's always best to select a designated driver. But let's deal with tour tastings and how to get safely to the next destination if there's only one person available to drive.

> **Side note:** Remember that in the Republic of Ireland and Northern Ireland they drive on the left side of the road. If this is an obstacle for you, I will cover some strategies for conquering this challenge later in the chapter.

Please Drink Responsibly!

We have all heard the tragedies that occur when people act irresponsibly by drinking and driving. You are not only endangering your own life but also the lives of your passengers and others on the road. Don't regret an error in judgment for the rest of your life.

Below, I have provided some guidelines for driving between distilleries—however, it's important to always use your best judgment. Remember that our bodies all handle alcohol differently, especially in smaller quantities. Know your limitations, and if you are planning on drinking beyond your tour, definitely make alternate plans to get from the distillery to your next destination.

The legal limit for blood alcohol content (BAC) in Ireland is 0.05% for standard drivers and 0.02% for professional drivers, learners, and driving novices. In Northern Ireland, the rule is no more than 80 milligrams of alcohol per 100 milliliters of blood, or 35 micrograms of alcohol per 100 milliliters of breath. The UK government suggests that if you are going to drink, you should not drive. They even warn you that some alcohol may still be in your blood the next day and it could endanger your license. I've heard it referred to as a zero-tolerance policy.

Of course, it can be difficult to know how much alcohol equates to these levels of blood-alcohol content, so if you do decide to drink you should do so with caution, and always be prepared to take responsibility for your decision and subsequent actions.

This is a serious matter and if you decide to drink, be prepared to take responsibility for the consequences of your actions.

Alcohol.org suggests that a female at 100lbs, consuming 35ml of 43% ABV whiskey and entering a vehicle five minutes after drinking would measure a blood-alcohol content of approximately 0.04%. However, it's important to understand that this is just an estimate and there is no guarantee your tour will stick to low ABV samples – in fact, most don't, and there are several tours where you will taste cask-strength whiskey that can rise to 75% ABV or new make that can be even higher. And, as I've said before, everyone's body handles alcohol differently. Then there are other factors to take into account, such as how long it has been since you last consumed a meal. If you question your status at all, get a taxi.

If you want to get a rough idea of how your height and weight affect your blood alcohol level, check out this calculator: alcohol.org/bac-calculator.

Take Mini Bottles

It's difficult to sit there watching others enjoy a sample, knowing you will have to wait. My technique is to bring three numbered mini bottles with me—I nose and take a small sip of the whiskey during a tasting and then pour most of the sample into one of the numbered bottles and enjoy them at my accommodations later that evening.

Ask if They Offer Driver's Packs

This has become standard practice in many distilleries in Scotland, but in Ireland, I only talked to a couple of distilleries that made driver's packs available. (With any luck, this will change in the near future.) Normally, a tasting will include three to five whiskeys, while a driver's pack may only be a single mini bottle offering, so taking your own mini bottles or asking if the distillery provides empties is preferable.

Carry Snacks with You

It's always good to have some type of snack that you can munch on in-between tours. Having food in your stomach can help reduce the effects of alcohol in your system, and it's a good way of getting food in your belly if you don't have time for a sit-down meal before your tour. Fast-food restaurants are rare in Ireland compared to North America; if you do have a meal before a tour, be prepared to ask for the bill as waiting staff are less aggressive than their American counterparts.

Sleep Near the Distillery

No, this is not suggesting you pull up some blades of grass outside the distillery to catch some z's. Instead, find a hotel or Airbnb within walking distance or a short ride-share from the distillery. That way, you won't have to worry about driving, and you can safely ride or walk back to your accommodations. I have even had a B&B offer to drive me to and from a nearby distillery. Note that this can be more difficult with rural distilleries.

Have a Backup Plan

Sometimes you will get caught up in the moment and consume more than you should. Always have a backup plan. Knowing there are taxis, trains, or buses available can keep you out of a lot of trouble.

SPECIAL DRIVING CONSIDERATIONS

For the uninitiated, driving on the opposite side of the road can seem intimidating, especially when you consider all the roundabouts and little towns you will face. When you finally commit to it, that first moment when you get into the wrong side of the car will remind you that this is going to take some patience and focus. Take a deep breath and stick with me here. Driving a rental through Ireland can be an incredibly rewarding way to travel. Here are a few things to consider that will help ease your mind and conquer your fears.

Get in the Right Mindset

Before I left for my first trip to Ireland and Scotland, I sat in my car, closed my eyes, and mimicked shifting gears with my left hand and visualized how I would handle turns. I got into the habit of "think left." I also went on Google Maps on my laptop, pulled up some streets I would take, and zoomed in to street level. Then I clicked up to intersections to see signage and got a visual of how to enter a roundabout and how to execute turns.

Roundabouts are Usually Easy

If you don't have a lot of roundabouts in your area, the idea of going into one from the opposite side may seem daunting, but in reality, roundabouts are usually well marked and in most cases you will follow traffic into them, so it is hard to make a mistake. That said, be careful of roundabouts in little villages. They can sneak up on you and signage can be difficult to spot. Just slow down and, in the rare case someone honks at you in frustration, just ignore them. Safety first.

Sometimes there are several roundabouts in a row. This can cause what I call "roundabout fatigue." Be careful of this as it can lead to you becoming frustrated and making rash decisions, like speeding into a roundabout to "get it over with." You never want to speed into a roundabout. Always take your time and look to the right to make sure no traffic is coming.

Stop Driving on the Shoulder

One of the most peculiar side effects of sitting on the other side of the car is the "shoulder" problem. Right-hand-side drivers aren't used to sitting so close to the center of the road. Suddenly, you will sense your car moving off the road to the left shoulder of the road. This may happen frequently on motorways. To solve this, find a spot in the bottom right area of your windshield and try to aim the road's center stripes into the corner.

Narrow and Single-Track Roads

It took three trips to Ireland and Scotland before I finally figured out that my left side mirror is my friend. To American drivers, the roads in Ireland can seem extremely narrow. Your body will seize up when you see a truck (or lorry as they call it in Ireland) coming down one of these narrow roads while you face a stone wall on the other side. This can feel like a real leap of faith until you look in your left side mirror and realize you aren't as close to the side of the road as you think. Take it slow at first—you will get used to it.

If you are using Google GPS, it loves to send you down as many single-track roads as it can find. These little lovelies can have you driving for a half a mile or more with no shoulder or pull off. If you meet oncoming traffic, one of you is going to have to back up: if you are coming down a hill, it is your duty to do the backing up; if you're on a flat surface and know you aren't far from a pull off, be courteous and back up, allowing the other car to pass. Driving on these types of roads is a negotiation, so don't be selfish.

If you want to avoid single-track roads, the best bet is to stick to the larger road ways. Many of the roads have a letter along with the number to give you a sense of the road's size. Here is a helpful guide for which ones you should take or avoid, depending on your comfort level:

> M roads are large motorways and are usually dual carriageways. These should be the easiest roads to travel.

> R roads are regional roads that can get narrow but are less likely to drop to a single lane.

> L roads are local so sometimes they are extreme. Sometimes you can't avoid them, especially with rural distilleries like Tipperary, Killowen, and Baoilleach.

Be careful of narrow one-lane bridges, which can sneak up on you in a hurry with little warning. Also, be careful of blind hills and curves on single-track roads. Take it slow and turn on your headlights when driving these smaller roads.

Think Left

As soon as I get in my rental car, the first thing I do is remind myself to think left. When I come up to roundabouts or turns, I think left (even on a right-hand turn, you will want to stay left on the road you are driving onto). If you are on a single-track road, remind yourself to think left as too much time on one can lead to forgetting where you are.

And if you make mistakes, don't dwell on them. Frustration creates an unnecessary distraction.

Speed Limits are a Suggestion

No, I'm not telling you to race through Ireland. Exceeding the speed limit is against the law. I say posted speed limits are a suggestion because you will quickly learn that people in Ireland go at their own pace. And rural roads can have quite a few twists and turns, so be careful about trying to match posted limits—use common sense. Often you will end up behind a large vehicle and end up driving half the speed limit. Amazingly, I found that Google GPS often works this into travel time estimates. Leave plenty of time between rural distilleries. You never know when a herd of livestock may end up blocking your path.

Also, don't speed up trying to make up for lost time. Those road signs with a camera icon are there to remind you that it doesn't just take an officer of the law to saddle you with expensive tickets. And don't think that because there isn't a camera sign you are free to speed. Some cameras calculate how quickly you traveled between signs.

Right Turns Will Be Your Biggest Challenge

If there is a creepy feeling I couldn't get over on my first trip, it was that sense I was going to get slammed into by oncoming traffic whenever crossing the highway with a right turn. Of course, no one is really coming at you; you will just have to get used to this.

Switching Countries

Travel between the Republic of Ireland and Northern Ireland is easy. In fact, you may not even notice you have switched from one country to the next. That said, be aware that the Republic uses the metric system (kilometers) and Northern Ireland uses imperial measurements (miles). Because I rented my last car in Dublin, the speedometer did not include miles per hour. If this happens to you (and hopefully it won't), it'll be up to you to calculate the speed differences in your mind. Also be aware that your rental agency will probably charge extra for driving between the two countries. It is best to pay this fee with your rental if you know you will cross the border (they may equip cars with GPS to alert the agency of any breach).

Side note: Some of the main motorways in the Republic of Ireland have tolls, so it's best to have some spare change in Euros for these. Also note that on the M1 heading south from Dublin Airport there is an automatic eToll area where they capture your license plate number and you are required to pay the fee by 8 p.m. the following evening. Check with your rental agency as they may have this fee built into the price of the car hire. Otherwise, head to etoll.ie/driving-on-toll-roads/information-for-visitors to find out how to make a payment. Don't forget, there are penalties for non-payment.

BY TAXI

Car-share services like Uber and Lyft are a wonderful addition to the traveler's toolbox. Unfortunately, as of this writing, Ireland does not allow hiring of privately owned vehicles; as I understand it, Uber's app does work in Ireland, but it will have you hiring a taxi.

If you need a taxi after a tour, it is best to ask an employee of the distillery. Taxi services range in quality and they should be able to give you the best option.

ON FOOT

I like to say that walking around in a country that drives on the opposite side of the road is more dangerous than driving there. When you are in a car, there are signs and other cars to guide you, but crossing a street can feel very different, especially because we get very comfortable looking one direction first when doing so. Always be aware and take extra care when crossing. Towns often mark crosswalks to remind you.

Accommodations

There are a variety of lodging options throughout Ireland and Northern Ireland. My advice would be to choose your accommodations based on the location of your last tour of the day.

BED & BREAKFASTS

This is my favorite option. Here you meet the proprietor of the bed-and-breakfast, get some personalized information on things to do in the area, enjoy a comfortable night's rest, and then wake up to a meal to fuel the day. If you are a meat eater, I highly recommend the full Irish breakfast. This will provide protein for the entire day and you can lean on snacks to keep you going until your evening meal.

There's a wide selection of B&Bs scattered throughout both countries, most of which can be booked through your favorite Online Travel Agents (OTAs) like Hotels.com, Booking.com, and Kayak.com.

AIRBNBS AND HOME RENTALS

Home rentals can be an inexpensive option, and are often located much closer to rural distilleries than more traditional lodgings. I have found some exceptional rental accommodations in cities and near significant attractions; on my last trip to the Giant's Causeway and Bushmills, I was able to park at my accommodations and wander down to the causeway for an evening stroll. Search for options on airbnb.com, HomeAway.com, and FlipKey.com. Some OTA's now include home rentals as well, but watch the fees, as they can add up quickly!

HOTELS

If you are staying in Dublin, Belfast, Cork, or Galway, a branded hotel might be a nice, easy option. However, when you are traveling to distilleries deeper into the country, branded hotels are almost non-existent. Using an OTA to book means you should be able to spot where hotels might be located right alongside B&B options, so you can choose which works best for you.

CARAVANNING AND CAMPING

Caravanning (the Irish equivalent to RVing) is a fantastic option for those wanting to camp like the locals. There are a variety of parks throughout the island and you can also use websites like ireland.com to find great places to park. The only drawback may be if you are also planning to visit some city-based distilleries. In that case, you will need to find a bus, train, or taxi as a travel option. Many caravanning sites also have space for campers with tents. Glamping in Ireland is another option, while wild camping is a little more tricky. Do some web searches to see if there is something that fits your interests.

ON-SITE ACCOMMODATIONS

The good news is that some distilleries, such as Slane Castle and Echlinville, are now building out on-site accommodations. The bad news is that they are not quite ready yet. Just be patient: this will be an incredible option in the future.

Side Trips

Variety is the spice of life. Don't just cling to distilleries when you are in Ireland and Northern Ireland. There are a ton of fun places to see and explore. Maybe you are into nature, castles, adventure, shopping, or just incredible scenery and road trips. You will find all of that and more on the Emerald Isle.

To make your planning even easier, I have suggested side trips in the distillery profiles. Choose your favorites from the suggestions.

Here are some examples of fun non-whiskey experiences:

- Giant's Causeway
- Ring of Kerry
- Killarney National Park and Muckross House
- The Book of Kells and Trinity College
- Kilmainham Gaol
- Powerscourt House and Gardens
- The Rock of Cashel
- Titanic Belfast
- Kinsale Dining
- National Museum of Ireland
- Blarney Castle and the Blarney Stone

If you are bringing along children or someone who isn't as into Irish whiskey as you, you will thank me for suggesting these diversions.

COOPERAGES

The one thing missing from standard distillery tours is the experience of seeing a fully functioning cooperage. Barrel making is an amazing craft and something that would make an excellent addition to your time in Ireland.

If you upgrade to the Old Midleton Distillery "Behind-the-Scenes Tour," this takes you into a cooperage and goes through the barrel making process. If you are headed to Connacht Distillery or Achill Island, Dair Nua Cooperage in County Mayo doesn't have a formal tour, but they will host guests who request to visit via cooperage@dairnua.com.

Kentucky's Independent Stave is building a cooperage in Ireland, but there hasn't been a mention of a visitor's aspect. If Nephin Distillery is open to visitors during your visit to Ireland, they are considering including a cooperage in their facility.

WHAT ABOUT IRISH WHISKEY FESTIVALS?

Another great way to experience the best of Irish whiskey is to attend a festival. A festival enables you to go to a single location and sample many different whiskeys – from those on offer from the larger manufacturers to discovering new tastes from smaller craft distilleries. And, because they're all in one location, you won't have to worry about driving from distillery to distillery.

If you are planning to head to a festival, you'll need to plan months ahead; some sell out quickly and lodging fills up fast.

Here are the two big whiskey festivals in Ireland:

June: Dublin Whiskey Live (Dublin, IE)
whiskeylivedublin.com

July: Belfast Whiskey Week (Belfast, NI)
belfastwhiskeyweek.com

The Day of Your Tour

Here is a quick list of considerations for handling the day of the tour, being a good tour guest, and preparing for the consumption of alcohol:

- Eat before you drink.
- Bring some water. These tours can include stair climbing, hills, and walks through hot facilities, so you will get thirsty quickly.
- Try to take your time when tasting. Some tastings will feel rushed. Remember, you don't have to drink all that they offer. If you don't like one, move on. However, if a distillery only provides a single tasting glass, you might have to ask if there is a place you can pour out your sample.
- Should you buy at the distillery? If there is an opportunity to bottle your own, like at Tullamore D.E.W., or to get a distiller's special edition, then go for it. As for pricing inside and outside the distillery that varies from place to place. Also, be aware that some Irish whiskey may only be available in Ireland and/or Northern Ireland.
- Don't shy away from extended tasting experiences; many of them are worth the extra cash.
- Be prepared with questions for your guide. Nothing is more boring than a tour group that just tags along for the ride. Ask about the differences between their process and other distilleries. If they make pot still or grain whiskey, find out what their mash bill is. Ask how long their fermentation process is or what their favorite whiskey is—you might find out your tour guide prefers another brand! This book should provide you with plenty of ammunition in the way of questions.
- Bring some tip money and thank guides that do an extraordinary job. I know these tours are getting more expensive, but a great tour guide who shows passion and makes your day by providing a memorable experience is worth €2 to €5 or more.

Keeping Track of Your Plans

Congratulations! You are officially prepared to plan out the entire course of your Irish whiskey experience. Give yourself a little pat on the back. Then start firming up the distilleries you want to visit each day by plotting them out.

One thing that can help immensely is starting a document with each day of your trip set as a headline. I prefer Google Docs because I can always access them from my phone or laptop—just make sure to download an offline version. Then fill in your desired tours and times under each day's heading.

Next, fill in side trips and then find your accommodations for each evening. Time out the distance between each distillery and put in enough time between to allow for driving or transportation and breaks.

I like to wait on pulling the trigger on any kind of reservation until after I have a solid plan for each day. This way, you don't waste time changing them when a better arrangement develops. Start by making sure you can secure the transportation and passport you need to get to Ireland. Then, book your distillery tours by using the "More Information" links in each distillery profile. If the distillery provides one, add the confirmation number for your tour to the document. Place all of your hotel and car rental confirmations on this same document to make sure you have easy access if you need it.

DEALING WITH MONEY

If you are new to dealing with currency exchange and credit card use abroad, I have a couple of suggestions.

Contact Your Bank

If your bank or credit card company is unaware that you are traveling, they could put a stop to your foreign transactions; contact them in advance so they know to expect them and so you don't get cut off from your funds.

ATMs vs Cash Exchange

The best place to get money is from a trusted ATM. You will find ATMs all over Ireland and Northern Ireland—in convenience stores, petrol stations, outside banks, and inside supermarkets. Know that you will probably be charged a fee by your bank and from the ATM. It's worth always having around €100 or £100 on hand in case a distillery or merchant doesn't accept your credit card, or in case you need to pay for tolls on the highway.

Visa and Mastercard are the easiest to use in Ireland, while American Express and Discover can be hit or miss. Remember too that cash advances on credit cards can be expensive, so it is best to avoid this if possible. Always make sure you know your pin number on any credit or debit card: Europe uses a chip-and-pin system and if you still have an old-school card without a chip (the U.S. has been slow on this), you may be required to sign a receipt.

Dealing With Fees

If using your cards abroad, look for travel-friendly ones that don't charge foreign transaction fees. Some cards not only save on fees, but can also provide additional air miles, and travel protections—especially on rental cars.

Travel Checklist

If you're like me, just the logistics of getting to the airport and making sure I pay the bills ahead of time is enough to consume my focus. And, as someone who has worked over the years to overcome a very scattered mind, I live by checklists. In fact, if you were at my house, you'd see a small slip of paper by the door with the basics of what I need to consider each day when heading off to work (lunch, phone, laptop, bottle of water, etc.).

With that in mind, here is my general checklist of items and tasks. These give me ease of mind and confidence I have everything I need for a successful getaway. This list does wonders for cutting down that "oh crap" feeling I get when I'm five minutes from the airport and an hour from my house! I hope this helps you too.

Depending on your own circumstances, of course, you may need to make adjustments to this list. I also would suggest having a staging area somewhere in your home where, up to a week beforehand, you start collecting the items you need to pack. There is nothing worse than realizing you forgot some small but very important things, like your power outlet converters or your International Driving Permit, even though you thought about them three days before you left.

FOR BASIC SURVIVAL

- Easy-to-carry baggage. If you can get down to one bag, that is ideal.
- Up to five days' worth of clothing, remembering that you are packing for Ireland weather, not your home-base weather. A jacket or hoodie is essential all year round: Ireland has a cool climate and sudden downpours are the norm.
- Shaving accessories, toothbrush, toothpaste, and general toiletries.
- Suntan lotion (in summer).
- Liquids under 2oz. if possible; some items are acceptable up to 3.4oz.if you are taking them on-board the plane.
- Sunglasses.

- Laundry detergent, if you are staying over five days and have access to a washer and dryer. Coin laundry establishments are available in larger towns. There are outdoor facilities called Revolution Launderettes throughout the Republic, use at your own discretion and check reviews.
- Provide your itinerary, with contact numbers, dates and locations, to someone staying behind. Check in with them from time to time while you're away.
- Travel insurance. Although it might seem like an extra expense, this will cover your costs if the airline loses your luggage, you are delayed, or you have any issues with your belongings while you are away.
- Health Insurance. This is a must for me whenever I am away from my home country. A health emergency can ruin more than just your vacation. For a minimal cost, companies like Alliainz and GeoBlue (Blue Cross Blue Shield) offer a variety of affordable plans.
- COVID-19 vaccination records (if applicable).
- Download any handy apps. WhatsApp is popular for making calls over Wi-Fi in Europe. I also find Google Maps works great as a GPS, but use the download maps feature if you're going to be driving in remote areas. If you are using your cell phone for GPS, make sure your plan includes international data at a reasonable rate.
- Take any prescriptions (and plan to have any necessary checkups before you leave). Take an extra set of contact lenses or glasses, if possible.

LEGALLY

- A valid passport, good for the time you are going to be there and maybe a few months extra to be sure. U.S. and European citizens are required to have a valid passport to enter the European Union and the United Kingdom. A visa is required for extended stays, work trips, or for people from certain other countries.
- If you are renting a car, get your International Driving Permit and bring it with you. Your home country license will also be required. In the U.S., AAA offices offer international licenses for a small fee.
- Make sure, if taking kids, that you have their proper passports and a letter of consent if only one parent is traveling.

MONEY

- Contact your banks to inform them you'll be using your credit and debit cards overseas.
- See if your bank has any agreements with overseas banks to reduce fees on ATM transactions, and find their locations ahead of time, if possible.
- Though it's best not to carry large amounts of money, it's good to have some cash in case places you visit don't accept credit cards.

FOR WORK

- Laptop or tablet with chargers.
- Smartphone with chargers.
- Outlet converters (Ireland and Northern Ireland use the Type-G adapter). Don't get caught with no way to plug in your equipment. You can order these on Amazon. Also, European outlets work at 220 volts versus 110 volts; make sure your electronic equipment can handle this increased voltage.
- Make sure you have bills paid through your trip or that you can make payments securely wherever you are going.
- Set up an International plan with your phone carrier and make sure it's turned on. Use airplane mode or shut off data if you're going to be charged for it. Remember, apps like Google Photos may backup on your data plan unless you turn that off. Make sure all the countries you are going to are in your plan and be aware of any charges you may incur. If you aren't sure if your phone has recognized the transition from Ireland to Northern Ireland, rebooting the phone can sometimes help.
- Put a hold on your mail.

FOR HOME

- Take care of pets.
- Put a timer on any frequently used lights to have them pop on and off at normal times (to make it appear you are home).
- Put mail on hold and suspend delivery of newspapers or any other items that could collect on your lawn.
- Ask trusted neighbors to keep an eye out for any suspicious activity.

FOR LODGING AND TRANSPORTATION

- Plane tickets both to Europe and within Europe.
- Hotel reservations and a printout of confirmation numbers (or access through your phone).
- Everything you need for your car rental. Check the fine print on your agreement before you travel and make sure you pack all the documentation you need – some agencies will change your rate if you can't provide everything. Note that some credit cards will provide insurance for car rentals.
- Rail-pass reservations (you should buy your pass before you head to Europe).
- International Driving Permit (if you rent a car, this is essential and costs as little as $20).
- Some kind of GPS if you're driving.
- For Americans, I highly recommend getting the TSA Global Entry Pass with TSA Pre-Check. This will save time and frustration at the airport, including speeding up re-entry. Plan extra time at Dublin Airport when returning to the U.S. as customs inspection has moved from post-flight to pre-flight.
- Make sure you are not carrying any restricted items on the plane.

- If driving, get familiar with the rules of the road and signage differences in the countries you will be visiting. If you have never driven on the left-hand side before, or if you have never driven a manual transmission, pay the extra and get an automatic transmission in your car rental.

FOR ENTERTAINMENT

- Reservations for any shows, restaurants, or attractions you want to see (double check if the ones you want to go to require them, especially during the busy season).
- Headphones, any adapters and music or movies on your laptop, smartphone or tablet.
- Camera, if not using a smartphone. Or take an inexpensive backup that you can hand to someone without worrying about it being stolen.
- Memory cards for camera and battery charger.
- Use social media with caution while on a trip. Make sure you aren't broadcasting your absence to people who might take advantage.

Again, your list may vary. But I hope this is a great help in getting you on the road with peace of mind. Scribble any additional notes that pertain to you on these pages (it is your book, after all). It can help with any return visit to Ireland.

Now there is nothing left to do except prepare our palates.

PART THREE

WHISKEY TASTING PREPARATION

~~~~~~~~~~~~~~~~~~~~

"May your glass be ever full,
May the roof over your head be always strong,
And may you be in heaven
Half an hour before the devil knows you're dead."

- Irish toast

PART 3
Whiskey Tasting Preparation

When heading to Ireland for a whiskey adventure, there are those that long to learn the whiskey-making process, while others love the stories and distillery histories. The one thing we can all agree on is our desire to try some amazing spirits.

However, if you just head to the Emerald Isle and start knocking back those little samples mindlessly, then you will miss a great opportunity to dig deeper into what makes each of these whiskeys unique.

While each distillery will have its own way of telling you how to enjoy their whiskey, it's worth knowing that all distilleries will pour your whiskey straight from the bottle, with nothing added to dilute it. For the uninitiated, this can lead to a sensory overload and a lost opportunity to reveal the deeper character of the whiskey. This is how tastings become more about experiential characteristics like smooth, harsh, or intense, rather than about the flavor profile. If you are used to wine tasting, whiskey tasting is going to be more aggressive.

So rather than having you throw away these valuable tasting opportunities, I created the following pages to give you preparation tips and strategies to help you take full advantage of your Irish whiskey experience. This way you can be more present during your initial tastings and make informed decisions on which whiskeys you should buy, and which to recommend to friends.

TO ICE OR NOT TO ICE

The way you drink whiskey is a personal choice. Here are the ways you can get the most out of the spirit.

Neat

If you want to enjoy an Irish whiskey the way the distiller envisioned it, then order it neat. Some people find this the hardcore way to enjoy a whiskey, but an unadulterated pour provides a greater chance to discover mouthfeel and delicate undertones that are masked when adding ice or cocktail ingredients.

With a Splash

While neat has its place, a splash of water in whiskey can reveal a whole new sensory experience. The heavier the oils in an Irish pot still whiskey for instance, the more water can break that up and unveil hidden flavors and aromas that are just waiting for a chance to surface.

On the Rocks

For those that love the taste of whiskey and want to cool down on a hot summer's day, adding two or three ice cubes will do nicely. Adding ice is also a good way to introduce yourself to the taste of Irish whiskey without overloading the senses.

In Cocktails

When you think about mixing Irish whiskey with something, most likely you will think of an Irish coffee. Yet there are so many more Irish cocktails waiting to be discovered, such as the Irish Buck, the Tipperary, or an Irish hot toddy.

As most whiskey distillers and tour guides will tell you, the whiskey is yours so enjoy however you like. I agree with that sentiment, mostly. But a 27-year-old Redbreast might be a bit too pricey for something you are going to dilute in a cocktail. Still, if you have money to burn or you feel that whiskey is the only way you can achieve the perfect cocktail, go for it.

Just remember when you go to a distillery for a tasting, your only two options are likely to be neat or with a splash. I would say almost 100% of distilleries handle whiskey tastings this way for their core range.

And this is the very reason I want to use this opportunity to help you prepare your palate for a stronger spirit.

But before you grab a bottle to try, let's make sure we have the right tool for the job.

THE DRINKING GLASS

Just like a scientist or doctor, you will need the right equipment to create a consistent environment for a proper tasting. For the whiskey enthusiast, this will be the drinking glass.

To me, the tumbler (AKA the rocks glass, old-fashioned glass, or lowball glass) is the perfect vessel for whiskey on the rocks.

But for Irish whiskey-tasting tours, there are three styles of drinking vessels typically available.

The Glencairn

Created by Glencairn Crystal Studio Ltd. in Scotland, the company developed these glasses as a sturdy replacement for the stemmed tulip or copita glasses traditionally used by master distillers. Since their introduction to the market in 2001, full-sized and miniature Glencairn glasses have quickly become the industry standard world-wide for distillery tastings.

The Túath

Created by Irish Whiskey Glass, Ltd. in Ireland, as an iconic Irish whiskey glass, its base resembles the rocky shape of Skellig Michael, a rocky island off the coast of the Kerry peninsula. The flared top gives the glass an elegant look. With its larger size, this glass is versatile—designed to work as both a sipping glass and a drinking glass.

Mini Cups

It is likely some distilleries will use disposable cups. This became more prevalent during the Covid-19 pandemic. These can make getting the full tasting experience a wee bit more difficult, but still serve the purpose.

The Glencairn and Túath are sturdy enough that you might carry one with you when you travel. The advantage of these glasses is that their shape concentrates the vapors of the whiskey on the nose, giving you a better chance of picking up specific aromas during a tasting. I recommend the Glencairn or mini-Glencairn for the novice, as these bring the whiskey closer to the nose without obstruction. And, as you will learn in a moment, smelling whiskey is a major part of the tasting experience.

These glasses sell from anywhere between €15 and €20 each; you can find them in specialty shops, on Amazon, and through other online retail resources.

HOW TO TASTE LIKE A PRO

Now that you have some whiskey and your Glencairn whiskey glass, it is time to learn how to approach the aromas and taste of a whiskey.

Pour some whiskey into your Glencairn glass. This is not a drinking contest: you should only put enough whiskey in the glass to draw out two to three tastes. Remember, on the tours you are likely only to get around 10 milliliters of whiskey in your glass.

Side note: If you are sampling an aged whiskey, a little-known secret is to let the whiskey rest for one minute for every year it was in the barrel. All Irish whiskeys will be at least three years old, so letting the whiskey sit for a few minutes before drinking it will give the spirit plenty of time to settle in your glass. Whiskey experts suggest that spirits evolve as they breathe: the more refined your palate becomes, the more you will experience these subtle changes in your whiskey.

Start by picking your glass up by the base, not the bowl. Often you will see people hand warming their whiskey by cradling the bowl. In the world of cognac, the theory is that heat releases aromas in the spirit. While the same may be true for whiskey, the goal here is to standardize the environment. You won't have time at the distillery to warm your whiskey, so to have an apples to apples comparison, keep the whiskey at room temperature. Save the experimentation for when you are enjoying a more substantial sample while sitting around with friends. This warming concept can make for an interesting discussion.

Raise the glass to your nose. Place your nostrils near the lower edge of the glass, inside the bowl. The glass should not be touching your face, but should be within a half inch. Open your mouth slightly and breathe in lightly with both your nose and your mouth. Vapors from the whiskey enter your mouth and interact with your taste buds, adding to the nosing experience. Take in an easy breath at first. If you forcefully take in a whiff of stronger or less refined Irish whiskeys, you will burn your nostrils with the alcohol vapors. Smelling and tasting require patience and focus.

So what did you smell? If you just said whiskey, that is okay. It takes time and experience to discover specific scents. The smells you will find initially are usually the ones you are most familiar with. For instance, if you love green apples, that might be the first scent that jumps out at you. But you may think you can't smell anything at all.

Don't overwhelm yourself. Start by trying to identify a single basic scent. Most Irish whiskeys spend time in ex-bourbon oak casks, so smells like vanilla, toffee, or a nutty oak may be present. Others spend time in sherry casks, which might bring more raisins and dark fruits. See if you can spot something you recognize. If not, no worries. It took me months to catch distinct scents because I had never really paid that much attention to smells in the past. As I discovered a new scent, I started smelling it in more and more whiskeys. This is a skill that takes time to develop.

Don't drink yet. Take the glass away from your nose and swirl the whiskey gently in the base of the glass. Watch as liquid clings to the inside of the glass. We refer to these oily strands as the legs of a whiskey. The legs can indicate a higher proof whiskey and can also give a visual representation of the mouthfeel that you can expect (I'll get to that term in a moment). Thicker legs reveal a higher alcohol content and heavier mouthfeel. After rolling it, give the whiskey another nosing to see if the aromas intensify or if it uncovers something new.

Also, note the color of the whiskey. The longer a whiskey remains in a barrel, interacting with the wood, the darker its color. It can also be affected by higher proofs or additional aging in finishing barrels that were previously filled with another spirit, like sherry or port wine. However, it is not beyond some producers to add e150a caramel coloring to their whiskey. This is within the rules of Irish whiskey because it isn't supposed to change the flavor. That said, it is basically burnt sugar, so take that claim with a grain of salt. Normally, distillers add color to help create a consistent presentation or to give a sense that the whiskey is older. The more you learn to appreciate whiskey, the more you will find this color unnecessary and even a hindrance to understanding what is in your glass.

Now for the tasting. Bring the glass up to your face. Breathe in lightly through your nose and mouth as the whiskey slowly reaches your lips. Remember, your nose and mouth will work together to give you the full flavor experience. Put just enough whiskey on your tongue to coat it. This first sip is not where we analyze and seek flavor notes; this is only an attempt to shock your tongue to prepare it for the tasting. Alcohol is an unnatural element that takes some getting used to. It might be slightly unpleasant for a moment. But just think of it as a little pain before pleasure.

Now we are ready for the official taste. But before we move forward, let me explain where to focus your attention as you start your analysis.

Nosing

Now that you have had your initial intake of whiskey, see how the nose (smell) evolves from your first experience with it. Sometimes this second taste will reveal new aromas. Remember to breathe in with your mouth and nose while the liquid prepares to enter your mouth.

The Palate

Try to put into words the flavors and sensations you experience when the whiskey first hits your tongue. Do any flavors jump out at you? Is there a heavy alcohol bite, or is it a smoother experience? Does the initial flavor have an impact or is it subtle or non-existent? Most tasting focuses on the hard palate in the middle of your tongue and the soft palate in the back. However, I think the third and most overlooked area of the mouth is what I call the side palate. Focusing on this area can reveal new and fascinating flavors.

The Mouthfeel

To me, this is one of the most interesting and underappreciated variables in the tasting experience. It is part of the reason I have ditched the habit of putting ice in my whiskey. Each whiskey has a certain viscosity. A heavy whiskey, rich in oils, will lay heavy and thick upon the tongue, creating a silky or milky feeling. By contrast, a thinner whiskey will wash away quickly, leaving a less impressive experience. I have several whiskeys where the mouthfeel is what I look most forward to.

An interesting byproduct of determining mouthfeel is that you will start noticing the body of other liquids. Even different waters can feel lighter or heavier on the tongue.

The Finish

Think of this as the whiskey's aftertaste. Some whiskey burns as it goes down the throat. This happens more with grain whiskeys or whiskeys with a high alcohol content (or if you drink it too fast).

If you want to tame this effect, try holding the whiskey in your mouth a little longer. This dilutes the whiskey and allows it to go down easier. If it is also burning your tongue, consider taking a smaller sip next time or add a little water.

You should also try to sense which flavors stick and which disappear quickly during the finish. Some whiskeys have a long finish and others a short one. It is all part of the tasting experience and, as a whiskey taster, you will find your own preferences.

Side note: The term 'smooth' has become a convenient crutch for inexperienced tasters. Unfortunately, Irish whiskey has been a big promoter of this generic term. To quickly develop your palate, start looking deeper and determining what it is about the whiskey that makes you call it smooth. Is there less of a burn? Does the whiskey have a well-rounded experience from palate to finish? Or does it have a nice silky mouthfeel? The more you dig beyond generic terms, the sooner you become a whiskey aficionado.

EXPERIENCE YOUR WHISKEY

Okay, it is time for the analysis. Bring the whiskey back up to your lips and this time take a more substantial amount of alcohol into your mouth. You should experience much less burn than you did the first time, and the initial flavors should be more prominent on your tongue.

Get your mouth fully engaged with the whiskey. Use the hard, soft, and side palates to your advantage. Move the whiskey around your mouth and note how the flavor changes. Bourbon fans will recognize the name Booker Noe of Jim Beam. He has an interesting way to get his mouth engaged in a whiskey—a chewing motion he calls the Kentucky chew. Some people get a little overenthusiastic with this technique, and it turns into a noisy whiskey sloshing contest. There is no need to be overaggressive. Just work that whiskey around and focus on the flavors it reveals.

On the top of your tongue, you get a genuine sense of the mouthfeel. Sit with it there for a couple of moments. Then, as you roll it to the sides of your tongue, you will notice other flavors and sensations unveiling themselves.

There is a myth about how we have taste sectors on our tongues with sour, sweet, bitter, umami, and salty taste buds in specific areas. Unfortunately, this isn't true. That said, individuals may find certain flavors having more impact on different areas of the tongue. The sides of my tongue reveal spices, while many people experience them on the back of the tongue.

Also, as you move whiskey around your mouth, vapors travel to the back of your mouth and up through your nasopharynx into your nose. Even with your mouth closed, your nose is still helping you determine flavor profiles. This is why whiskey can taste flat if you have a stuffy nose. You also have taste buds on the roof of your mouth and down your throat. See how flavors change as you move whiskey around your mouth and after you swallow it. If you want to hear more about how we taste, check out the *Whiskey Lore Stories* podcast Season Two episode *Tongue Map and How We Taste Whiskey*.

The tour tasting is an excellent opportunity for you to share your flavor experiences and compare with others. But remember, the sensations aren't always the same for everybody, so don't feel you are wrong if you are experiencing something that no one else does—or if others are catching things you aren't. We have each experienced a unique variety of foods and smells in our lives and we each respond differently to certain tastes and scents. For instance, I love black licorice and might seek it out in a whiskey; someone else may not like that flavor and they will avoid a whiskey that has it.

You may also notice different cultural or regional references in tasting notes. In the United Kingdom and Ireland, you will often hear people talk about sherried whiskeys tasting like Christmas cake, a term unfamiliar to most Americans. I find many Irish pot still whiskeys have a graham cracker taste. This is a very American reference and may get some confused looks while you are in Ireland. Think of what flavors make up a graham cracker—grain and honey. This can help you translate your tasting experience to someone unfamiliar with your reference. It will also help you become a better taster.

How long should you hold the whiskey in your mouth? Well, some whiskeys will scream at you, "swallow me!" But others will be pleasant and you won't want to let them go. When you are trying to keep that whiskey in your mouth, your saliva will dilute it while you are attempting to savor it, which may make it easier to hold on to. I would suggest that ten seconds might be enough for you to pick out the most pronounced flavors. But if it takes 20 seconds, then stick with it.

If you are doing the tasting at home, this is where you can have a larger sample size and sit and enjoy sip after sip to get the full story. I have several whiskeys in my collection that seem to unveil something new every time I drink them. For me, these complex, multi-dimensional whiskeys are like new lands waiting to be explored.

As you swallow the whiskey, pay attention to any physical sensations and how long the flavor lasts in your mouth. This is what they call "the finish." These are all the different factors a professional taster will focus on. And what it will show you is that whiskey is more than just a beverage—it is a heavily nuanced experience.

For your third and final taste, go through the same process. If you like, add a couple of drops of water before sampling to see if that changes the experience and opens up any other flavors you might have missed.

TAKE NOTES

A great way to speed your education on Irish whiskey is to keep tasting notes. Get a little booklet or set up an online document where you can keep track of:

- The name of the whiskey
- The date you drank it
- The amount of water added
- What you smelled on the nose
- The flavor on your palate
- The mouthfeel
- The finish (what was the physical sensation? Did any flavors linger?)
- The overall impression

Then, next time you try the same whiskey, ignore your notes and start a fresh set.

What you will find is that, as your palate becomes more trained, you will pick out new flavors and understand what you find pleasing and off-putting in each whiskey.

You will also feel encouraged as you see the progress in your ability to pull out flavors and aromas. My ability to taste has undergone an incredible transformation since my first distillery tour.

Taking notes will enhance the growth of your knowledge and will give you more confidence in tasting and talking about what makes a specific Irish whiskey the right choice for you.

THERE IS NO NEED TO BE OVERWHELMED

When I started my whiskey drinking journey, I had plenty of doubts about my tasting ability. It was part of the reason I went to 19 distilleries on my first trip. I wanted a crash course so that I could stop sounding like a whiskey newbie. And that trip was an incredible learning opportunity.

Here are the two major lessons I learned during that trip:

Tasting is a Skill

Imagine that you want to be a great actor or athlete. Do you think you can just walk onto the field and instantly compete? No. Even those born with natural abilities still need to learn how to harness their powers. There are no overnight successes. Everyone pays their dues; some just get there faster than others. And some achieve their goals through sheer will.

Tasting whiskey is no different. No one gets it the first time they try it. It takes time to learn how to do it properly and to build experience with different flavors and styles.

If you love to cook or are a foodie, your experience with flavors and scents may give you a jump on the rest of us, but it will still take time to learn the unique flavors and aromas of whiskey.

The goal of your first trip should not be to come back as a master, but to gain your first steps toward mastery. Whiskey is a journey—and the journey is good. Make sure you enjoy it.

Smelling and Tasting are Specific to the Individual

Reading other people's tasting notes or hearing them from a tour guide or friend can be helpful for a beginner trying to get a handle on some basic flavors and scents present in whiskey. But tasting notes are training wheels and eventually you need to trust yourself. There are no wrong answers when it comes to your tasting experience. If you taste it, then it exists for you. If someone else doesn't taste the same thing, so be it.

USING OTHER PEOPLE'S TASTING NOTES

The Power of Suggestion

Be careful of continuous use of other people's tasting notes as a crutch. If I tell you something tastes like licorice or green apples, the power of suggestion may force you into finding those two flavor notes. Your brain will zero in on what you want it to find. And you may end up missing something no one else would have caught.

As you begin developing your tasting skills, relying too heavily on someone else's tasting notes can stunt your growth and limit your experience. Start by creating your own notes first then, if you choose, use another person's review to compare and contrast with your own experiences.

Reading other people's tasting notes can be extremely valuable to your growth, and in helping you to discover new whiskeys, so I am not suggesting to ignore them completely. But reserve accessing them until after you have established your initial relationship with a whiskey. Don't let them be the last word on what your tasting experience should be.

If I listened to others entirely, I might never have found a passion for certain whiskeys. My own reasons for enjoying an Irish whiskey are the things that will keep me coming back to it—not someone else's opinion.

Use the Experience You Have

Consider this: I can tell you something tastes like elderberry, but what if you have never had elderberry? How can you relate to my reference? And how will you ever find it in a whiskey?

We are all exposed to different foods and experiences in our lives. No two people are exactly the same.

For instance, I haven't spent my life around individual baking spices, so if you told me something smells like allspice I wouldn't know what you mean, so there would be no way that I could pick it out in a whiskey.

However, the first time I heard someone suggest allspice in a nosing, I went out and bought the spice, and took a sniff for myself. To my nose and experience, it reminded me of Russian tea. So now, when I smell certain whiskeys, if I smell Russian tea, I realize I'm smelling allspice.

So relax and know that all good things come with time and experience. And don't be afraid to rattle off some bizarre tasting notes. You never know where they might lead.

Side note: *The more you learn about tasting whiskey, the less important star ratings and grading scales become. You soon discover that what is a five-star whiskey to one person is a two-star whiskey to someone else. I have heard it said there are no bad whiskeys. I don't know if that's true, but I will say that beauty is in the eye of the beholder. Look at online and store ratings with a skeptical eye and read the flavor notes and comments instead. At least that way you can get a feel for what people like or dislike specifically about the whiskey. When I do my own YouTube tastings, I give my impression as an afterthought. To me, that is the least important part of helping you understand a whiskey.*

THE ART OF DISCOVERING FLAVORS AND SCENTS

So how can you simplify finding flavors and aromas on your own? Starting with one or two flavors is the best way. For me, apples and a nutty character seem to be the easiest to discover. If raisins and toffee are easiest for you, develop your awareness of them in a whiskey. Seeking one or two smells or tastes initially will keep you from sensory overload. And don't freak out if the scents or tastes don't come to you immediately. When you find one, write it in your notes. Next time you try the same whiskey, dig a little deeper. And if a whiskey seems hard to nose or taste, consider changing to a smaller glass.

As you develop your nose and palate, you will discover diversity in certain flavors. When you say cinnamon, are you talking about the Red Hots candy or the baking spice? When smelling vanilla, there are several variations. I try to think of what it reminds me of. Am I smelling vanilla-scented candles, vanilla extract, or something else? If it is an apple smell, is it an apple pie, green apple, or candy apple? Scents can be surprisingly diverse. Once you make a connection, it can help you spot that scent more consistently.

I equate it to that moment when you buy a certain model car and then suddenly see that model everywhere. It's a case of connecting your senses to a frame of reference.

> **Side note:** *So who is adding these flavors to your whiskey? That is just it. No one is—at least not in the way you would normally think. These scents and flavors occur naturally through the combination of grains, distillation, and the influence of maturation in a virgin oak cask or used bourbon or sherry cask. For instance, the vanilla comes from the vanillin found in the oak. Charring and barrel influence help bring this flavor note to the bourbon, which then finds its way into Irish whiskey. Distillers can increase fruitiness by allowing longer fermentation times, while pepper and spice can come from an increase in the unmalted barley content of the mash bill. Every part of the process has an influence on the flavor.*

THE FLAVOR WHEEL

Something that can assist your tasting and smelling progress is a flavor wheel. These handy little guides can be a big help to the beginner, who does not know where to start with finding flavors and scents.

To develop your nose and palate, start at the very basics in the center of the wheel and further define each flavor by working your way to the outside edges of the wheel.

WHISKEY LORE
FLAVOR WHEEL

To get a printable color copy of a flavor wheel, head to *whiskey-lore.com/flavorwheel*.

WHO JUDGES QUALITY? YOU DO!

One of the best parts about learning to taste and smell whiskey is no longer being beholden to other's opinions of what makes a quality spirit. After a few distilleries in Ireland and some experimentation at home, you will have the confidence you need to judge what you feel is a quality whiskey and what you would rather pass on.

Here are some things I learned by taking the training wheels off and developing my palate:

Age Ain't Nothin' but a Number

It is amazing how many people get sucked in by age statements. But there are several important factors that can influence the quality of a whiskey that rests for a long time in a barrel.

In Scotland, where 12 years is an average starting point for a whisky, the temperature doesn't change much from season to season, so the barrel is slow to impart its influence. Kentucky in the United States is notorious for its wild temperature and weather fluctuations, so whiskey ages and evaporates much faster there. The more it evaporates, the more influence the barrel has on its flavor.

Because of the young nature of the distilling industry in Ireland, you won't find many long-aged whiskeys. This doesn't mean they are inferior to scotch. In fact, some types like peated whiskeys or pot still whiskeys actually show more of their character at younger ages.

If you are a fan of the oak influence, and you like a nuttiness in your whiskey, then an older whiskey might be perfect for you. But if you like the fruit and other flavors that come from the original new make, then a long age might actually work against you. However, in Ireland and Scotland, the different types of used cooperage may also keep and soften the hard edges on those fruity notes, creating a nice subtle yet complex whiskey.

The placement in a warehouse and the size of the barrel can have a huge effect on the aging process.

Don't fall into the trap that older is better. It is just different.

Price Ain't Nothin' but a Number

Today whiskey has become extremely popular and a secondary market has developed where whiskey prices are heading into the hundreds, thousands, and even millions. Everybody seems to buzz about the latest Macallan release or Pappy Van Winkle bourbon. If you want whiskey as a collectible, maybe it is worth four figures to you. But how does Pappy Van Winkle taste? Is it the absolute best whiskey for your individual palate? Or are you just buying it for status or because someone said it was good?

I am picking on Pappy because it is one of the most sought-after bottles on the market— and yet probably 95% of the people who want it have never tried it.

Educate yourself. Sample it if you get a chance, but there is no need to buy a bottle just because it has an elevated price. If a bottle of €20 Paddy Irish Whiskey does it for you, use the thousands of dollars you saved and start a college fund for your child. Or take a trip to Scotland, the U.S., or Japan to see how the rest of the world makes whiskey.

SUPPLEMENT YOUR LEARNING

If you are struggling early on, it is fine to check out some YouTube videos where people do tastings and product comparisons. In mine, I try to educate you on a certain aspect of the whiskey or its history while doing the tasting. Check out a variety of channels. You will see what whiskeys others have a passion for and you will find some common threads in tasting notes.

Go to **whiskey-lore.com/influencers** to see my latest list of whiskey tasters and groups from around the world. And also, see some of my tasting videos at **youtube.com/whiskeylore**.

AFTER YOUR IRISH WHISKEY EXPERIENCE

Another great way to learn is to hold a whiskey-tasting party. Get three or four close friends, ask each to bring three bottles of whiskey—a higher priced, a mid-priced, and a quality bottom-shelf bargain. That'll give you nine to 12 whiskeys to taste. Sit around and discuss each one. Notice how the power of suggestion makes its way around the room. Each person will pick out their own flavors and suddenly you will detect those same flavors and experiences yourself.

Try to introduce your friends to some whiskeys you are curious about but haven't tried yet. I used to always try to sneak in a Canadian whisky or blended scotch just to see if anyone would bite. People are still unfamiliar with a lot of Irish whiskeys, so you will have a secret weapon in your arsenal after your trip to Ireland.

Here are some other great ways to share your love of whiskey:

Food Pairings

Once you have done a chocolate and whiskey pairing, it is hard to shake the temptation to experiment further. Find some fun combinations and host a chocolate and whiskey pairing event of your own. Or find some great food pairings and host a guided whiskey and food pairing dinner party.

Local Events

There are plenty of whiskey-tasting festivals circling the United States and across the globe. Do a quick Google search for "whiskey festivals" and see if you can find something happening in your area. Also check out local pubs and restaurants that host whiskey-tasting events.

Meetup

Seek whiskey fans in the area through services like *Meetup.com* and *Facebook groups*, or start your own.

Find Local and Regional Distilleries

I like to encourage people to try a variety of whiskeys to expand their palates. In the United States, there are plenty of styles to experiment with. Don't just stick to Kentucky bourbon, try rye whiskey, American single malt, Tennessee whiskey, and bourbons from across the country. See what your country produces. Germany, France, Australia, Japan, and many other countries have seen rapid growth in their whiskey offerings. The same tasting techniques apply, so go see what your local craft distillery has come up with.

Plan Your Next Adventure

Make another trip back to Ireland or maybe expand into Scotland, Canada, the United States, or even Japan.

Whiskey can create a lifetime of experiences. Let me be the first to welcome you to this wonderful world of whiskey. If you haven't done so already, it's time to jump into the profiles and start picking out the distilleries that will make your Irish whiskey experience unforgettable.

PART FOUR

PROFILES: YOUR GUIDE TO IRISH WHISKEY DISTILLERIES

When planning a great adventure, having tons of information at your fingertips can make all the difference to how easily your journey comes together. But if the information you collected is in various formats and varying degrees of quality, it can bog you down.

When I started putting together my first whiskey adventure, I read through articles and blog posts, looked at bottles in the liquor store, read whiskey tour tips on blogs, and asked anybody I could for advice. Most of the time, the information was scattered and limited.

I created this guide so that you can quickly get to the heart of what each distillery is known for. I also wanted to provide a fast and easy reference guide to help you easily plan out each day's adventure without having to do a lot of hopping between websites.

I hope you find this guide invaluable. And if you do, please help spread the word by leaving a review on Amazon or by sharing how helpful it was on social media, and with your friends and family. Your reviews and support will help Whiskey Lore grow into a resource for whiskey travel and history all over the world.

Thanks for giving me your trust.

How to Use These Profiles

In this section, you will find full profiles for the 27 Irish whiskey distilleries that offer a visitors' experience. I have visited every one of them: what I am providing is a mix of reference information and my personal experience. These are not quality reviews of the distilleries; instead, I am guiding you with the valuable information you need to determine which distilleries fit your personality and what to expect when you visit.

I have broken the distilleries up into logical regions. In addition to the 27 main distilleries, I have also included further distilleries to consider at the end of each region. The Irish whiskey industry is growing at a rapid rate and I want you to be aware of distilleries that are opening soon, don't have regularly scheduled tours, or open for special events and private tours, as the situation can change quickly—many of the distilleries I write about in these sections will no doubt join the other 27 in future editions of this book. Keep them in mind and, if they sound interesting, put them on your wish list and check their websites when making your final plans. You might be one of the first to experience them firsthand.

The five regions (Dublin, Midlands, Northern Ireland, North Atlantic Way, and South) are covered in Part 2 (Conquer a Region).

You don't have to read this guide from beginning to end. Skip around to the distilleries that catch your eye. If you have trouble finding the brands you are interested in, check out the appendix at the end of the book for a handy brand-to-distillery cross-reference.

Within each two-page full profile, you'll find the following information:

ABOUT

This part of the profile features information about the facility, the distillery's history, and basic details about the tour. This is not comprehensive; I wrote these to give you an initial impression of the distillery. My job is to get you interested in finding the ideal experience. If you want more of the distillery's marketing focus, check out their website.

It's important to stress here that distilleries will occasionally change their offerings, especially the whiskeys served during the tastings. Use this area as a loose planning point, but do not be disappointed if what they offer has changed.

LISTEN/WATCH FOR

Every distillery tour has something that makes it unique. I want to give you a chance to keep an eye out for these cool features or stories when you visit. Like going on a treasure hunt, this feature will give you something to look for that others might miss.

GETTING THERE

Using GPS is your best bet for directions, but here I provide some tips on parking and special considerations when heading to the distillery.

TOUR DAYS

One of the most frustrating parts of using distillery websites for planning is constant age verification and clicking through website cookie agreements while trying to figure out tour times. I would have given anything to just flip back and forth between pages to get general tour times.

I have provided the days of the week that tours are running, but not hours. As of this writing, many distilleries are just opening up to a full schedule. Because of the constant change in hours available, it is best to use the website for exact times, but this feature will allow you to get your days of the week lined up.

SIDE TRIPS

We cannot live by whiskey alone. Each distillery profile features one or two diversions that will help you see more of Ireland and Northern Ireland than just pot stills and tasting rooms. Your traveling companions will thank you.

CLOSEST DISTILLERIES

For each distillery, I provide two further distillery suggestions that are in close range to the one being profiled. This can save a lot of plotting out on maps during your initial search. Note that I am only referencing the 27 distilleries that are currently offering visitor experiences.

AT A GLANCE INFORMATION

I wanted you to have important information at a glance. Besides distillery information, you will also find basic details based on the standard tour experience.

The information below the distillery profile photo includes:

Featured Brands

This is a list of the distillery's whiskey brands. It doesn't mean they distilled them at the distillery or that they will be available to sample but rather to give you a sense of what brands are associated with that distillery. I have made these lists as comprehensive as possible.

Use the brand index in the back of the book to find an alphabetical listing for all distilleries.

Whiskeys+

Each distillery offers its own selection of whiskey and new make styles. They may also offer gin, vodka, rum, or poitín. If you have a particular style of whiskey you are interested in, this feature will help you find the distilleries innovating with the classic Irish pot still style and the ones making single malts, grain whiskeys, and blends.

Some or all of the whiskeys a distillery offers may be sourced from a third party. This is a temporary measure until their own spirits reach three years of age or until they feel they are ready to be released. Sourced spirits come from high-quality distillers like Great Northern, Cooley, Bushmills, Midleton, and West Cork. Many distilleries age and finish these whiskeys for an additional period to put their own spin on the liquid. Never hesitate to ask if they source a particular whiskey—most distilleries are transparent.

I have provided the date of a distillery's first barrel being filled (where applicable) to help you anticipate when their first spirits will reach maturity. But remember that distilleries don't always release their spirit as soon as it officially becomes whiskey.

Available to Tour

Each distillery features different parts of the process in their tours. If you love smelling the angel's share like I do, then make sure the distillery features "warehouse" as an option.

The areas of the distillery I highlight include:

- Malting
- Milling
- Lab
- Fermenters
- Column Still, Pot Still, Hybrid Still, Lomond Still
- Warehouse
- Bottling

Understand that extended tours are available at many distilleries, and they may include areas of the distillery not shown here. These listings are all based on where the standard tour goes.

Tour Cost

Distillery tour prices are subject to change, so rather than giving specific prices, I have used a symbol (free—€€€€ or ££££) to signify a price range. See Part 2 (Making Your Final List) for the corresponding prices for each symbol.

I have also included details about driver, senior, minor, and children's discounts. Remember, children aged eight and under may not be allowed to tour.

Website

This is a link to the home page of the distillery's website.

Location

This is the address for the distillery and where you need to head for the tour; I've included postal codes where possible, as this is the best way to find a distiller in Google Maps. If you aren't able to locate the distillery, find maps at *whiskey-lore.com/distilleries* or use the quick link at the end of each profile.

DREW'S TOP THREE REASONS TO VISIT

This is as close as you will get to a review. I wanted you to have a sense of the things I thought set one distillery tour apart from another. If you are having a hard time choosing between two distilleries, this information might help tip the scales in the right direction.

MORE INFORMATION

This link to the distillery's Whiskey Lore Profile page will provide basic information about the distillery. Want access to each of these distillery profiles online? Sign up for a membership on *whiskey-lore.com/signup*, log-in, and then go to the direct links given here to have access to maps, tour-booking links, the ability to add the distillery to your own personal wish list, and find profiles from my other books. It will help you keep all of this information at your fingertips wherever you travel.

While making your list, I would encourage you to stretch yourself like I did. Mix and match between well-known and craft distilleries. I found some excellent tours at distilleries I had never heard of. The older distilleries may be more polished, but the new guys can show you entrepreneurial spirit and innovation.

Have fun looking through these profiles. Irish whiskey is right at your fingertips.

Dublin Whiskey Distillery Map

1 **DUBLIN LIBERTIES DISTILLERY**
2 **PEARSE LYONS DISTILLERY**
3 **ROE & CO. DISTILLERY**
4 **TEELING DISTILLERY**
5 JAMESON BOW STREET DISTILLERY

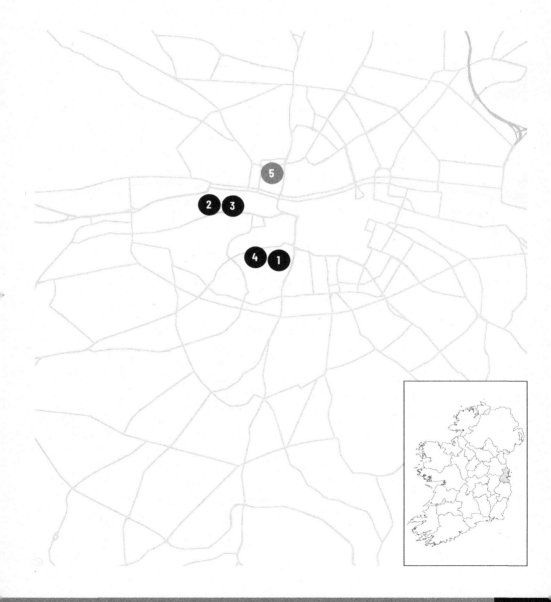

Dublin Liberties

ABOUT DUBLIN LIBERTIES

Are you someone who embraces the grittier side of history? The Dublin Liberties Distillery has just what you are looking for. Built in a 400-year-old mill and tannery, this building lived through the historic whiskey boom of the 19th century, and also survived the Great Dublin Fire of 1875 when streams of burning whiskey flowed through the streets of the area of Dublin known as the Liberties.

This tour is rich with stories that will light up your imagination. Your guide will introduce you to the working class of the past, their tenements, stories, and legends. And while you listen, enjoy a sample of a unique honeycomb liqueur and the distillery's flagship whiskey, The Dubliner. Next, you will learn their production methods and how they got their magnificent stills inside the building. You will finish with a guided tasting of a single malt and blend in their world-class bar.

The Dublin Liberties expressions embrace the rich stories of the area with names like Oak Devil, Murder Lane, and Copper Alley. The initial spirits were sourced and aged through the expertise of Bushmills veteran Darryl McNally. He was also on-hand during the development of the distillery and his experience shows on the new make I sampled. As their in-house whiskey reaches maturity, it will slowly make its way into their lineup.

LISTEN/WATCH FOR

As you will learn on your tour, the Great Dublin Fire is a reason distilleries in the city don't offer trips to a warehouse. Listen for why you don't use water to extinguish a whiskey fire. Then find out the ingenious and somewhat disgusting way the firefighters halted the blazing river of whiskey.

GETTING THERE

The area's public transportation system is handy, but Dublin's Golden Triangle of distilleries are easily accessible on foot. Make sure you have Google Maps handy on your smartphone, as this isn't on a major thoroughfare. If you want to park, the safest way to avoid a car clamp is to head to the parking garages at Thomas Street or St. Stephens Park.

BASIC TOUR

Daily (it is advisable to book weekday tours four days in advance)

SIDE TRIPS

- **The Book of Kells at Trinity College** Tour one of Ireland's great treasures, and visit an incredibly beautiful historic library that dates back to 1732.
- **Irish Whiskey Museum** Here you can explore the history and lore of Irish Whiskey, perfect if you're new to it. At the end of the tour, enjoy whiskey samples and step into the cafe for a cocktail.

CLOSEST DISTILLERIES

- **Teeling Distillery** (NW-0.17 km)
- **Roe & Co. Distillery** (NW-1 km)

At A Glance

BRANDS	Dead Rabbit, Dublin Liberties, The Dubliner
WHISKEYS	Pot Still, Single Malt, Blend
FIRST BARREL FILLED	2019
AVAILABLE TO TOUR	Milling, Fermenters, Pot Still
TOUR COST	€€ — Senior, Student, Child Discounts
WEBSITE	*thedld.com*
LOCATION	The Mill, 33 Mill St, The Liberties, Dublin 8, D08 V221, Ireland

Drew's Top Three Reasons to Visit

1   I absolutely love how this distillery embraces the darker side of the Liberties past. Walking in, I saw a sign that said "Welcome to Hell." It made little sense at first, but the stories help to connect the dots.

2   While they sourced the whiskeys I tasted here, they were exceptional and the new make was fruity, malty, and very sippable. The future looks bright for their transition to their own in-house made spirits.

3   This historic location on a backstreet gives you the feeling you are experiencing the Liberties of old, without the infamous smells that might have pervaded it when it was filled with tenements.

MORE INFORMATION: *whiskey-lore.com/dublinliberties*

Pearse Lyons Distillery

ABOUT PEARSE LYONS DISTILLERY

Visit the only distillery in Ireland, or the world, built into an 800-year-old church and surrounded by a graveyard. Religion and whiskey have always had a connection, with distillers of the past supporting the maintenance and construction of churches. Here, Pearse and Deirdre Lyons' passion project makes that connection more palatable. Starting with a derelict church, they added a beautiful glass spire, and upgraded the inside while installing Kentucky-built pot and hybrid stills.

The tour starts with a tasting while the late founder introduces himself on a video and the video's narrator tells the history of the church. Next, the group gathers in the graveyard to hear stories of some of its inhabitants, including Pearse Lyons's own grandfather. Once inside the church, you will learn what it takes to preserve a historic building like this. As your guide walks you through the whiskey-making process, they will describe how the beautiful stained-glass windows relate to that process.

Next, a second guide will walk you through the experience of nosing and tasting a whiskey. When choosing your ticket, you will also choose how much you taste and will receive a wristband that will match you up with the barrel head where your whiskey rests. At the tour's end, take a few moments to enjoy some photo opportunities with the stills.

LISTEN/WATCH FOR

The St. James's Church graveyard has an astronomical number of bodies buried in it. Find out how many and, as you look around, try to figure out how they got them all in there. If your guide doesn't mention it, this is a great opportunity to ask.

GETTING THERE

As with many distilleries in Dublin, you can easily walk from one to the next. Save steps by taking the easily accessible buses. If you're driving, you may find limited parking on Crane Street, or you can use the garage on Thomas Street.

BASIC TOUR

Wednesday through Monday

SIDE TRIPS

- **Guinness Storehouse at St. James Gate** The Liberties were known for more than just the Big Four distillers. Here you have the chance to walk through the history of Ireland's world-famous Guinness Irish Stout and to pour your own pint. There is a marvelous 360° view of Dublin at the end of the tour.
- **Kilmainham Gaol** Experience the darker side of Dublin history by visiting this historic jail. Built in 1796, it housed some of Dublin's most notorious criminals and hosted the executions of those that stirred up the 1916 Easter Rising

CLOSEST DISTILLERIES

- **Roe & Co. Distillery** (E-0.25 km)
- **Jameson Bow St. Distillery** (NE-1.3 km)

At A Glance

BRAND	Pearse
WHISKEYS+	Single Malt, Blend, Gin
FIRST BARREL FILLED	2017
AVAILABLE TO TOUR	Milling, Fermenters, Pot Still
TOUR COST	€€ — Senior, Student, Child Discounts
WEBSITE	*pearselyonsdistillery.com*
LOCATION	121-122 James's St, The Liberties, Dublin, D08 ET27, Ireland

Drew's Top Three Reasons to Visit

1 You can tell Dr. Lyons's love for both whiskey history and the history of this area; it resonates throughout the entire tour.

2 Thanks to its sister distillery in Kentucky, visitors on both sides of the Atlantic get to experience the craftsmanship of another country. Town Branch in Lexington features Scottish pot stills, while Pearse Lyons here in Dublin features Kentucky's own Vendome pot and hybrid stills. You can even sample a Kentucky single malt.

3 Would it be wrong to call this a "religious experience"? The storytelling and connection to the church's past is top-notch.

MORE INFORMATION: *whiskey-lore.com/pearselyons*

Roe & Co. Distillery

ABOUT ROE & CO. DISTILLERYS

Roe & Co. might not be a familiar name to you, but at one time the Roe family's Thomas Street Distillery was the biggest producer in Ireland—when Ireland ruled the whiskey world. Today, Diageo, the largest distiller of scotch whisky and owner of Guinness, has brought this famous name back to Dublin with a modern twist.

As you await your tour, catch a sneak peek of the still room from ground level. Your guide will walk you through the history of the Roe family and brand before giving you a bird's-eye view of the stills. From there, you will learn about and taste Roe & Co's flagship blend. Next, the tour diverges along a choice of paths depending on the ticket you purchased. One tour walks you through the blending, while the other lets you craft your own cocktail. This hands-on experience is a rarity in the world of distilleries and gives this tour a leg up on its neighbors.

There are plenty of opportunities for photos along the way and your tour ends with a complimentary cocktail in the bar. This will give you the rare opportunity to view the bones of the building, which is a former Guinness power station. A look through the window reveals the stark contrast between the beautiful reconstruction work and what modern workers created out of it.

LISTEN/WATCH FOR

As you look at the front of the distillery, notice the unique color of the brand's logo. Listen during your tour for the reason they chose this specific color.

GETTING THERE

The two optimal ways to reach the distillery include walking or riding bus 123. There is street parking available nearby but make sure you're aware of the rules in order to avoid a wheel clamp. You can also use the car park on Thomas Street.

BASIC TOUR

Thursday through Sunday

SIDE TRIPS

- **Bar 1661** If you are curious about Ireland's native spirit, check out the best poitín bar in town. I highly recommend the Belfast Coffee (Bán Poitín from Echlinville, cold brew coffee, demerara sugar syrup, cream, and nutmeg) for those wanting a hot beverage.
- **St Michan's Church** There has been a church on this spot since the 11th century. One of its unique highlights is the burial vault filled with mummified remains. This was a favorite attraction of author Bram Stoker

CLOSEST DISTILLERIES

- **Pearse Lyons Distillery** (W-0.25 km)
- **Jameson Bow St Distillery** (NW-1 km)

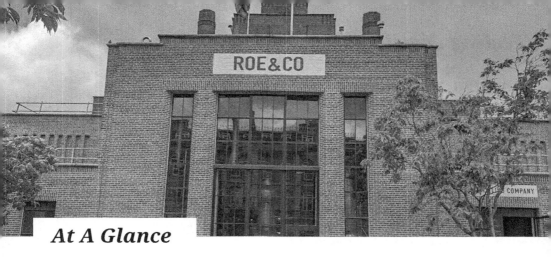

At A Glance

BRAND	Roe & Co
WHISKEY	Blend
FIRST BARREL FILLED	2019
AVAILABLE TO TOUR	Fermenters, Pot Still
TOUR COST	€€€
WEBSITE	*roeandcowhiskey.com*
LOCATION	92 James St, The Liberties, Dublin 8, D08 YYW9, Ireland

Drew's Top Three Reasons to Visit

1 If you enjoy a hands-on experience, Roe & Co. has something for both the whiskey lover and inspired mixologists. Learn the art of blending with the Blending Experience and finish with an Old Fashioned. For cocktail lovers, learn the five primary flavors and choose one for the cocktail you will create. Both experiences include a tour of the distillery.

2 You will get a superb view of the historic George Roe windmill. At one time, it was the tallest in Europe. As you take photos, your guide will walk you through the glory years of the Thomas Street Distillery, which once produced over two million gallons of whiskey a year.

3 If you are planning to visit the Guinness Storehouse at St. James Gate across the street, this distillery makes the perfect partner to complete the experience.

MORE INFORMATION: *whiskey-lore.com/roeandco*

Teeling Distillery

ABOUT TEELING DISTILLERY

Teeling helped lead the way for the new breed of Irish distilleries. When Jack and Stephen Teeling came to Dublin to start their operation in 2012, it had been 125 years since anyone built a distillery in the Liberties. The brothers look to capture the best of the past while injecting fresh energy into Irish whiskey. The result is an innovative distillery that uses a combination of styles, barrel aging, and finishing techniques to create interesting and inviting whiskeys.

The tour begins with the story of Dublin's whiskey past and how the industry fell on hard times. Then you quickly shift to an introduction to the brands, styles, and expressions that are bringing world recognition to the distillery and its spirits. A walk through the distillery provides insights into how they whiskey and the art of maturation. Because Teeling has been around for a while, your tasting will include some of the longest aged whiskeys produced by the new generation of distillers.

If you are planning to visit multiple distilleries, Teeling is the easiest one to plan around, offering tours as frequently as every 20 minutes. There are also flexible tasting experiences. The lowest-price tour features a sample of their Small Batch whiskey and a cocktail. If you want to extend your tasting, the higher-priced tour features a sample of the flagship whiskeys and two distillery exclusives.

LISTEN/WATCH FOR

When the brother's ancestor Walter Teeling ran the Dublin based Marrowbone Lane Distillery in the 19th century, he left his name off the distillery. However, the Teeling's names are all around the current distillery. Listen for individual family members' names and where they ended up.

GETTING THERE

To get around Dublin, I highly encourage the purchase of a Dublin Bus pass. But Dublin is also a very walkable town. Either way, you can make a day of it without worrying about getting behind the wheel. If you want to drive in, the safest way to avoid a car clamp is to head to the parking garages at Thomas Street or St. Stephens Park. Either way, it is good to have a GPS feature available on your smartphone to help you find these off-the-beaten path distilleries.

BASIC TOUR
Daily

SIDE TRIPS

- **St. Stephen's Green** A wonderful place to stretch your legs while enjoying sculptures, gardens, and the fountain. Add shopping at nearby Grafton Street to your stroll.
- **The Little Museum of Dublin** Learn the history of Dublin in as little as a half hour by taking a guided tour of this fun little museum. Be aware that there's limited space, so tours sell out quickly.

CLOSEST DISTILLERIES

- **Dublin Liberties Distillery** (SE-0.17 km)
- **Roe & Co. Distillery** (NW-1 km)

At A Glance

BRAND	Teeling
WHISKEYS+	Pot Still, Single Malt, Grain, Blend, Poitín
FIRST BARREL FILLED	2015
AVAILABLE TO TOUR	Milling, Fermenters, Pot Still
TOUR COST	€€
WEBSITE	*teelingdistillery.com*
LOCATION	13-17 Newmarket, The Liberties, Dublin 8, D08 KD91, Ireland

Drew's Top Three Reasons to Visit

1 The recent boom in distillery start-ups in Ireland means many distilleries will feature younger whiskeys or only sourced whiskeys. Teeling's head start in the market allows them to be one of the few with well-matured spirits that have been produced on-site.

2 As you walk through the distillery, you will notice beautiful artwork everywhere. A local artist named Shane Sutton produced these stunning paintings.

3 The on-site Phoenix Café is an excellent place to drop in for a coffee or tea and a light lunch or snack. The food is prepared using locally sourced ingredients.

MORE INFORMATION: *whiskey-lore.com/teeling*

DUBLIN

Dublin Considerations

JAMESON'S DISTILLERY BOW STREET

Visit the grounds of the historic Bow Street Distillery. Built in 1780 by the Stein family, a young Scotsman named John Jameson and his bride Margaret Stein moved to Dublin to get into the family whiskey business. John was so successful at managing the distillery that he eventually took over ownership. Under his leadership, it became one of the most respected distilleries in the world, at a time when Irish whiskey was booming.

During the depression in Irish whiskey sales in the 20th century, Irish Distillers, LTD. abandoned this distillery for a new one down at Midleton. By the 1990s, owners Pernod-Ricard saw an opportunity to convert the old facility into a museum devoted to keeping Jameson's past alive, while stimulating brand awareness.

There are a variety of experiences available. The standard tour takes you through both history and process, and ends with a tasting. If you are new to Irish whiskey, the tours get high marks for entertainment value and the energy of the tour guides. For the history fan, Bow Street is the only opportunity to stand where the Dublin distillers of the 19th century stood.

Understand—especially if you're a hard-core whiskey fan—that this is not a working distillery. And, in the interest of full disclosure, I should point out that I haven't visited it myself, despite its popularity—but that doesn't mean I won't. It is a piece of history that needs to be preserved for future generations as a reminder of when Ireland ruled the whiskey world.

Website: *jamesonwhiskey.com*

Midlands Whiskey Distillery Map

1   **KILBEGGAN DISTILLERY**
2   **POWERSCOURT DISTILLERY**
3   **SLANE DISTILLERY**
4   **TULLAMORE D.E.W. DISTILLERY**
5   AHASCRAGH DISTILLERY
6   BOANN DISTILLERY

7   CHURCH OF OAK DISTILLERY
8   GLENDALOUGH DISTILLERY
      (UNDISCLOSED)
9   GREAT NORTHERN DISTILLERY
10   LOUGH REE DISTILLERY
11   OLD CARRICK MILL DISTILLERY

Kilbeggan Distillery

ABOUT KILBEGGAN DISTILLERY

For the whiskey history buff, a visit to Kilbeggan is a treat. This distillery is a well-preserved time capsule that catapults you into the 19th century, when it was known as Locke's Distillery. With a history that dates back to 1757, the combination of rich stories and the ability to walk in the footsteps of past distillers is an incredible experience. When John Teeling sold this distillery to Beam Global (now Beam Suntory) back in 2012, he counted it as one of the few regrets of his storied career; visiting, it's not hard to see why—it's a magical place.

The tour includes a walk through the historic distillery and the current small batch distillery. You will see the massive gears, water wheel, iron mash tuns, and fermenters. In the modern craft distillery, you will hear how two distillers work to keep the unique wooden mash tuns clean and the techniques used to produce the modern version of this working class style distillery. Who knows, you might even meet one of those distillers along the way.

As you head to the tasting bar, you will have the chance to sample from their selection of single malts, single grains, blended, and peated whiskeys. Check out the gift shop, snap some photos, and even bottle your own whiskey for an extra charge. If you are driving, ask for a mini bottle to store your tasting for later.

LISTEN/WATCH FOR

After being closed in the mid-20th century, a new still was needed when it re-opened in the 1980s. They purchased a historic still from another area distillery that had been shut down and mothballed. You can see that historic still on the tour. See if you can catch which competitor sold it to them.

GETTING THERE

The distillery is near to the M6, which, along with the M4, takes you from Dublin to Galway. When you reach the distillery, there is plenty of parking behind it. Just be careful at intersections as the locals may drive faster than you expect.

BASIC TOUR

Monday through Friday (pre-book)

SIDE TRIPS

- **Sean's Bar** What is a trip to Ireland without stopping off at a whiskey bar? Sean's ranks as the oldest public house in Ireland, dating back a thousand years!
- **Center Parcs Longford Forest** Looking for a family getaway? A stay here opens your access to a water park, interactive Gaelic games, biking, a spa, and restaurants.

CLOSEST DISTILLERIES

- **Tullamore DEW Distillery** (S-17 km)
- **Pearse Lyons Distillery** (E-90 km)

At A Glance

BRAND	Kilbeggan
WHISKEYS	Pot Still, Single Malt, Grain, Blend, Rye
FIRST BARREL FILLED	1757
AVAILABLE TO TOUR	Fermenters, Column Still, Warehouse
TOUR COST	€€ — Child Discounts
WEBSITE	*kilbegganwhiskey.com*
LOCATION	Lower Main St, Aghamore, Kilbeggan, Co. Westmeath, N91 W67N, Ireland

Drew's Top Three Reasons to Visit

1 The old Locke's Distillery is like stepping back into the 19th century. It will amaze you how well preserved the old distillery is. For the whiskey-history lover, this is as close to a "must see" as I can name.

2 In Kentucky and Scotland, it is the norm for distilleries to offer a keepsake as part of your tour. In Ireland, this is still rare. Perhaps it is their ownership by Beam Suntory that has inspired Kilbeggan to do the same. I received a nicely branded mini Glencairn at the conclusion of my tour.

3 There are plenty of photo opportunities around this distillery. Before your tour, take a walk out to the bridge on the main road. Here you can see the Locke's smokestack, the moss covered waterwheel, and get a splendid view of the exterior of the distillery.

MORE INFORMATION: *whiskey-lore.com/kilbeggan*

Powerscourt Distillery

ABOUT POWERSCOURT DISTILLERY

South of Dublin, near the base of iconic Sugarloaf Mountain, the once neglected Powerscourt House & Gardens is now a premiere getaway destination. Inspired by the resurgence of the Irish whiskey industry, the estate converted its nearly 300-year-old grain mill into a distillery visitor's center and café. With an eye on creating a premium whiskey brand, legendary distiller Noel Sweeney was brought on board to establish both the distillery and a top-notch reputation for its Fercullen whiskey.

The surrounding Wicklow Mountains, along with this historic estate, provide a smorgasbord of stories—some of which you will hear on the tour. Then, after a seven-minute video walks you through the whiskey-making process and introduces you to the area, you step out of the old mill into a fully functioning modern distillery. After viewing the equipment, you will do something you can't do in a Dublin distillery—walk among the casks in a warehouse. The tour ends with a tasting of three Fercullen whiskey expressions. And if you love going beyond whiskey, check out the website for weekend tours that include a food pairing.

Whether you are looking for a day or week-long, diverse getaway experience for the family, a place for a corporate retreat, a wedding event, or just a pleasant alternative to the hustle and bustle of Dublin, Powerscourt delivers.

LISTEN/WATCH FOR

Why is the distillery called Powerscourt and the whiskey called Fercullen? Keep your ears open during the tour for this detail and find out how the two names relate.

GETTING THERE

The drive to this distillery is beautiful. Located just 4 km west of the N11 highway (which runs from Dublin), it's an easy winding road up through the town square of Enniskerry to reach the hilltop entrance to Powerscourt Home & Gardens. When you arrive at the estate, go to the furthest point of the large parking lot and the distillery will be to your left. There is plenty of parking and the gardens and hotel are just a short stroll away.

BASIC TOUR

Wednesday through Sunday

SIDE TRIPS

- **Wicklow Heather Restaurant** The Writer's Room here is a must for literature fans, featuring first editions of Bram Stoker's *Dracula* and James Joyce's *Ulysses*
- **Powerscourt Estate** See the stunning Italian and Japanese gardens, plus visit the hillside pet cemetery

CLOSEST DISTILLERIES

- **Dublin Liberties Distillery** (N-26 km)
- **Teeling Distillery** (N-27 km)

At A Glance

BRAND	Fercullen
WHISKEYS	Single Malt, Grain, Blend
FIRST BARREL FILLED	2019
AVAILABLE TO TOUR	Fermenters, Pot Still, Warehouse
TOUR COST	€€€
WEBSITE	*powerscourtdistillery.com*
LOCATION	Powerscourt Estate, Enniskerry, Co. Wicklow, A98 A9T7, Ireland

Drew's Top Three Reasons to Visit

1 Located at the northern point of Wicklow Mountains National Park, the beauty here is undeniable. If you are looking to surround a distillery visit with other experiences, this is an excellent family-friendly option. Stay in a luxury hotel, visit the beautiful Italian-inspired gardens, and take a short drive to see Ireland's tallest waterfall—all in the shadow of Sugarloaf Mountain.

2 During your tour, you will get a nice sample food pairing designed by their in-house Food Historian & Food and Beverage specialist Santina Kennedy, a native of the region. If this is your thing, make sure you check the website for more extensive whiskey and food pairing events.

3 The youth of the emerging Irish whiskey market gives you few opportunities to taste longer aged whiskeys. Fercullen features several whiskeys with ages in the double digits.

MORE INFORMATION: *whiskey-lore.com/powerscourt*

Slane Distillery

ABOUT SLANE DISTILLERY

What goes better with whiskey than rock and roll? If you are a fan of both, this distillery has your vibe. In 1981, the grounds of Slane Castle were alive with the first of many concerts that would grace the banks of the River Boyne. The brainchild of Slane Castle's proprietor Lord Henry Mountcharles (known in Ireland as "The Rock and Roll Aristocrat"), the concerts led to the creation of a sourced spirit called Slane Castle Irish Whiskey. When the source of that whiskey dried up, the ultimate dream of opening their own distillery came true. With the help of Kentucky's Brown-Forman Company, a worldwide brand developed and a distillery was built out of the historic horse stables..

There are several ways to experience Slane Distillery. The Flavor of Slane Tour features a walk through the distillery, its history, processes, a tasting of two Slane expressions, and a chocolate pairing. If you have the time, the Amplified Tour takes you deeper and provides a highly recommended deconstructed tasting of the elements that make up Slane's flagship blend. They also have cocktail- and coffee-making classes available.

After your tour is complete, or if you don't have time for a tour, stop off in the bar where you can enjoy more sips and sit in booths creatively constructed out of former horse stalls.

LISTEN/WATCH FOR

There are several challenges to building a distillery inside a historic landmark; modifications have to be made so when they lower distilling equipment into the building, it doesn't damage or subtract from its historical elements. With that in mind, keep an ear out for the considerations that had to be made to bring their two pot stills into the facility.

GETTING THERE

Located 45 minutes north of Dublin on the N2, the distillery and castle are hard to miss. Check the website, or better yet, make an online reservation when you decide to tour. They lock the gate on days when the distillery is closed. You will find ample parking on-site.

BASIC TOUR

Thursday through Sunday

SIDE TRIPS

- **Battle of the Boyne Visitor's Center** Learn about the historic battle that changed the course of Irish history, enjoy walking the battlegrounds, and see original and replica weaponry.
- **Slane Castle** Just a short stroll from the distillery, learn about the famous concerts that take place here every year, see the beautiful furnishings, and look for special tours hosted by its current proprietor and the driving force behind the distillery, Alex Conyngham, the Earl of Mountcharles.

CLOSEST DISTILLERIES

- **Jameson Bow St. Distillery** (S-48 km)
- **Roe & Co. Distillery** (S 55 km)

At A Glance

BRAND	Slane
WHISKEY	Blend
FIRST BARREL FILLED	2018
AVAILABLE TO TOUR	Fermenters, Pot Still
TOUR COST	€€ — Child Discounts
WEBSITE	*slaneirishwhiskey.com*
LOCATION	N51, Slanecastle Demesne, Co. Meath, C15 XP83, Ireland

Drew's Top Three Reasons to Visit

1 Slane is one of my favorite Irish whiskey blends. On the tour, you will learn about the three elements that make up their whiskey and have an opportunity to buy a distillery exclusive bottling that highlights one of them.

2 This is a wonderful place to spend a day. Combine the distillery with a visit to the historic castle. In between tours, you can enjoy a tipple or an Irish coffee at the bar and check out the food options outside.

3 It is hard to deny the beauty of the grounds. As you enter the gate, there is a wonderful view of the River Boyne, Slane Castle, and the distillery.

MORE INFORMATION: *whiskey-lore.com/slane*

Tullamore D.E.W.

ABOUT TULLAMORE D.E.W.

In 2010, the makers of famous scotch brands The Balvenie and Glenfiddich expanded their portfolio and dipped their toes in the Irish whiskey market by purchasing the Tullamore Dew brand. Originating in the nearby town of Tullamore in 1829, its most famous owner, Daniel Edward Williams, got his start with the company as a stable boy in the mid-1860s. His impact was so great that his initials became an acronym connected to the distillery brand. During the last decade, owners William Grant & Sons enhanced that history by using capitalization to emphasize his initials. The current distillery was built in 2014 to move production from Midleton Distillery to 100% in-house.

Before you start your tour, check out the brand's fascinating history and enjoy a complimentary tea or coffee. There you will see how Irish Distillers Ltd. kept the brand alive during the major Irish whiskey downturn of the 20th century. You will also see a variety of historic bottles that include the long time slogan "Give every man his Dew."

The standard tour is an impressive 105 minutes long and features several tastings— including an Irish coffee, a tasting in the blending room, and a barrel tasting in the warehouse "snug." Along the way, you will learn the history, see the pot stills, and ride a mini bus through the distillery grounds; for an extra fee, you can even blend your own Irish whiskey.

LISTEN/WATCH FOR

Watch for the phoenix during your tour. This is the symbol of the current town of Tullamore, which was decimated by fire back in May 1785. The fire started when a hot-air balloon snagged a chimney and collapsed on residences; a determined town rose from the ashes. The balloon accident is thought to be the first air disaster in history.

GETTING THERE

This is one of the more easily accessible tours for drivers. It takes a spin on just a few roundabouts south of Tullamore to get you to the car park. There is a good amount of paved parking out front. If you have visited before, be aware that the tour is no longer in the old warehouse downtown.

BASIC TOUR

Tuesday through Sunday. Reservations are suggested as tours are limited to 8 people. Book online for a discounted rate.

SIDE TRIPS

- **Lough Boora Discovery Park** Rent bikes, see the sculptures, and explore the natural beauty of Ireland's heartland with your family.
- **Kinnitty Pyramid** Visit Egypt in Ireland with this 19th Century replica of the Great Pyramid of Giza. It is the final resting place of its creator's family.

CLOSEST DISTILLERIES

- **Kilbeggan Distillery** (N-17 km)
- **Pearse Lyons Distillery** (E-104 km)

At A Glance

BRAND	Tullamore D.E.W.
WHISKEYS	Pot Still, Single Malt, Grain, Blend
FIRST BARREL FILLED	1829
AVAILABLE TO TOUR	Fermenters, Column Still, Pot Still, Warehouse
TOUR COST	€€€ — Discount for online purchase
WEBSITE	*tullamoredew.com*
LOCATION	Ballard, Tullamore, Co. Offaly, R35 E027, Ireland

Drew's Top Three Reasons to Visit

1 It is rare that I suggest a mixed drink as part of my top three, but that Irish coffee is fantastic. It actually reminds me of a Guinness by appearance, but this decadent delight features a wonderful cream mixed with that distinctive whiskey and coffee blend.

2 While the price is a little higher than most standard tours, you definitely get your money's worth. And the Irish coffee experience, along with storytelling, helps to elevate this tour. If you were only able to visit one distillery in Ireland, this would be the one I would recommend for a well-rounded experience.

3 This is one of the only distilleries I've seen that actually has a separate set of three pot stills so they can keep their single pot still whiskey distillation separate from their single malt whiskey distillation. The pot stills are in a picture-perfect location in front of several windows and extremely well kept.

MORE INFORMATION: *whiskey-lore.com/tullamoredew*

MIDLANDS

Midlands Considerations

AHASCRAGH DISTILLERY

In the heartland of Ireland, the husband-wife team of Gareth and Michelle McAllister are building a state-of-the-art distillery from the bones of a historic mill. The project is intense and has required major renovations by experienced local contractors. Their goal is to have Ireland's first fully sustainable distillery by using solar energy, the old water wheel, and high-energy heat pumps with energy storage capabilities. The distillery will also bring renewed vitality and visibility to the community through employment and a high-quality visitor's experience.

With distilling starting in 2022 and a visitor's experience opening in 2023, this is a distillery to keep on your wishlist. There are two buildings underway: a brewhouse and a stillhouse, with a third due to be part of a future phase. Bottling, blending, and maturation are planned as a part of future tours. Meanwhile, their sourced whiskeys will give you a sense of the styles you can expect. They have spared no expense as their distillate will soon run through prized Forsyth stills. Check the website when planning to see if tours will be available during your visit to the area.

BRANDS	Clan Colla, Uais
WHISKEYS+	Pot Still, Single Malt, Blend, Gin
FIRST BARREL FILLED	TBD
TOURS	TBD (check website for updates)
WEBSITE	*ahascraghdistillery.com*

BOANN DISTILLERY

After 50 years in the Irish drinks industry, Pat Cooney set his sights on fulfilling a dream of opening a family-run distillery. He took the lessons learned during his long career and outfitted the Boann Distillery with equipment focused on creating a clean distillate. His three Italian copper pot stills are custom designed to do just that, allowing for optimal control over reflux and plenty of sulfite-cleansing copper contact.

Boann's current lineup of blended and single malt whiskies falls under the name "The Whistler." Inspired by Pat's incredible skill at whistling a beautiful tune, these sourced whiskeys are a bridge to distiller Michael Walsh's triple distilled Irish single pot still whiskey. The spirit of innovation and experimentation is alive and well here as recent projects with Irish-whiskey historian Fionnán O'Connor and Colorado distillery Talnua attest.

The distillery was built in an old car dealership. It features plenty of parking, and a wonderful view of the Boyne Valley, from whose legends it draws its name. It is easily accessible from the motorway that runs between Dublin and Belfast. There are plans for a full visitors' experience, including an on-site restaurant, tasting bar, as well as tours. Keep your eyes on their website when planning your trip. Who knows, maybe you will be one of Boann Distillery's first guests.

FEATURED BRAND	The Whistler
WHISKEYS+	Pot Still, Single Malt, Blend, Gin
FIRST BARREL FILLED	2019
TOURS	TBD (check website for updates)
WEBSITE	*boanndistillery.ie*

CHURCH OF OAK DISTILLERY

It is amazing how much of the grain that Ireland turns into whiskey comes from County Kildare—especially considering the area has been devoid of legal distilling for over a century. That is now changing as some high-profile investors are putting generous money into the development of the Church of Oak Distillery. The distillery's name comes from the English translation of the Irish word Kildare, and its whiskey will go far beyond a dependence on wood for flavor. The stills have been designed for the ultimate in flexibility, allowing double, triple, and two and a half times distillation. Every drop of spirit will flow through a worm tub that can help control the body of the distillate. There is even a Lomond still on-site that will allow for the creation of styles yet explored by Irish distilleries.

The distillery is being built into a historic mill, with its design such that it will be fully visible to tour guests and the processes fully transparent. This will be one of the rare distilleries that give you an eye into the casking of whiskey. Blockchain technology is being employed to track and store information on every drop of whiskey they make from seed to bottle. A distillery for the new generation of whiskey drinkers, Church of Oak will be groundbreaking, yet focused on the traditions that create the best of whiskeys. This is still an early project, so look for the distillery to open for visitors in the coming years—it will be well worth keeping on your radar.

FEATURED BRAND	TBD
WHISKEYS	Pot Still, Single Malt, others TBD
FIRST BARREL FILLED	2022
TOURS	TBD (Follow them on Instagram @churchofoak)
WEBSITE	*TBD*

GLENDALOUGH DISTILLERY

This was one of the tougher distilleries for me to catch up with. Despite having over a decade in the market, there isn't a distillery location to visit. This is on purpose. Like a lot of smart entrepreneurs, the friends who started Glendalough knew there was a need to raise revenue and create awareness for a brand before going to the expense of creating a visitor's attraction. Now that the whiskey is in over 40 countries and their gin has garnered a reputation for quality, the planning phase for the distillery is in full swing.

They are looking to build one of the most picturesque distilleries in Ireland to produce their gin and whiskey. They already own the land, near the Wicklow Mountains, and when complete this will be another distillery option for those looking to take a breather from the city life of Dublin. It will be a couple of years until they break ground, but it sounds like a distillery well worth waiting for. Stay tuned.

FEATURED BRAND	Glendalough
WHISKEYS+	Pot Still, Single Malt, Grain, Gin
TOURS	TBD (check website for updates)
WEBSITE	*glendaloughdistillery.com*

GREAT NORTHERN DISTILLERY

This is the home of the great John Teeling, the godfather of Irish whiskey. If you taste a sourced whiskey in Ireland, there is a good chance it comes from this distillery. This facility was the one time home of Harp Beer, but now churns out a wide variety of distillates. Unfortunately, this is not a tourable distillery. Still, if you make it to historic Dundalk, it's worth strolling by to see the outside of the historic brick offices and the stainless-steel mash tuns through the window. At the time of writing, the distillery had 340,000 casks of whiskey in bond and had just announced they are doubling the capacity to keep up with the demand for Irish whiskey.

FEATURED BRAND	Burkes
TOURS	No
WEBSITE	*greatnortherndistilling.com*

LOUGH REE DISTILLERY

Three siblings in Ireland's heartland had a notion to energize the future of their home-town, Lanesborough, by building a distillery. Their parents met as educators at the local tech school in the 1960s and Peter, Mike, and Sheila Clancy's memories are of growing up in a town once driven by the local power station. To create a spark in the area's economy, they secured buildings near the park and the River Shannon a couple of years back and have created a micro-distillery, with plans to build a larger distillery across the street.

Currently, they offer tastings at the micro-distillery where you can learn about the town and enjoy their sourced whiskeys, as well as the gins and vodkas they are creating. They are currently distilling small amounts of whiskey on-site, but full-scale whiskey distillation will wait for the larger distillery to be built, with plans for breaking ground in 2023. In the meantime, they are aging, blending, and injecting creativity into their blends. Bart's Irish Whiskey, named for their father, shows this creativity using a blend of five whiskeys, including a peated malt and malts finished in rye and Oloroso sherry casks. The lightweight bottle shows their focus on sound environmental practices. Call ahead for a tasting and plan for some leisure time at the nearby park; stop off for a hot beverage at the Lough Ree's Distillery Yard coffee stand. Also, if you are a fan of gin, check out their gin school in Dublin.

FEATURED BRAND	Bart's, Lough Ree Bridge Series
WHISKEYS+	Malt, Grain, Blend, Vodka, Gin
FIRST BARREL FILLED	2022
TOURS	Ask (check website for updates)
WEBSITE	*lrd.ie*

OLD CARRICK MILL DISTILLERY

The hillsides of Ireland's Ancient East are teeming with legends. It is in this idyllic country where Steven Murphy recently began searching for a home for a brand new distillery. As luck would have it, he stumbled upon a 300-year-old flour mill in need of some love. After researching it, he discovered the mill was once owned by Thomas Barton, an Irishman who left the mill and his homeland to establish a wine house and vineyard in the Bordeaux region of France. That wine house became the worldwide success known as Barton & Guestier. When Steven connected with B&G, they gifted 50 red wine casks for him to use when he produces his first whiskey.

While Steven awaits his license for whiskey distillation, he is sourcing and blending spirits under the name May Lóag. This curious name is from the Irish language and means "the one that stands out from the crowd." One look at the bottle and you will agree. It features diamond-cut glass and takes its inspiration from the decanters of the past.

The ambitious restoration of the mill is already underway and there are plans for a tasting room and visitors' experience. Check the website before finalizing your plans to see if tours have started.

FEATURED BRAND	May Lóag
WHISKEYS+	Blended, Single Pot Still, Single Malt, Blend, Gin
FIRST BARREL FILLED	TBD
TOURS	TBD (check website for updates)
WEBSITE	*oldcarrickmill.ie*

Northern Ireland Whiskey Distillery Map

1	BUSHMILLS DISTILLERY	7	GLENS OF ANTRIM DISTILLERY
2	COPELAND DISTILLERY	8	J&J MCCONNELL'S DISTILLERY
3	ECHLINVILLE DISTILLERY	9	KILLOWEN DISTILLERY
4	HINCH DISTILLERY	10	LIMAVADY DISTILLERY
5	RADEMON ESTATE DISTILLERY	11	TITANIC DISTILLERS
6	AN CARN DISTILLERY		

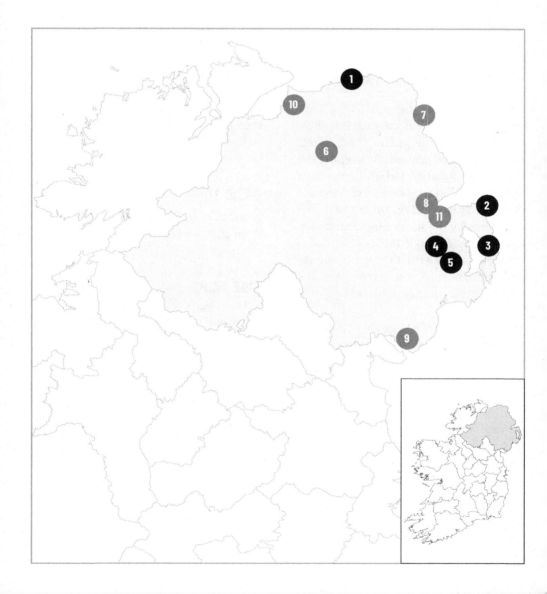

Bushmills Distillery

ABOUT BUSHMILLS DISTILLERY

Celebrated the world over as one of the most historic brands in whiskey, a visit to Bushmills is a rite of passage for *any* lover of whiskey, not just Irish whiskey. Established as a brand in 1784, this distillery not only saw the great Irish whiskey boom of the 19th century, but was also one of only two distilleries in the country to survive and produce throughout the great Irish whiskey depression of the 20th century.

Every tour guide here delivers their own knowledge and passion for whiskey, and reviews of guides at Bushmills show many are praised for keeping the experience lighthearted and fun. Even with my behind-the-scenes experience, I could sense that energy on my visit. The tour stops by the mash tun, fermenters, and travels through the still house. A standout is the visit to the warehouse and the explanation of barrels and the flavor profiles of their whiskeys.

The tour ends with a guided tasting in the 1608 Bar. Here you can choose to try other selections from the Bushmills lineup and distillery exclusives. It is also a great place to have your photo taken next to another piece of Irish whiskey history—the ornate copper pot still that was used at the now defunct Coleraine Distillery.

LISTEN/WATCH FOR

On-site barrel making is a rarity, especially in Irish whiskey. Yet this craft was once a staple of any sizable distillery.

As you enter the warehouse, look for a painting to the left that prominently features two men; these are Bushmills' third and fourth generation coopers.

GETTING THERE

Located an hour north of Belfast, Bushmills has a fantastic location within a short drive of the stunning landscape of Giant's Causeway. Several tour companies make their way up to the distillery and it is a favorite stop during the annual North West 200 motorbike race. Located at the southern end of the village that shares its name, the distillery is hard to miss. There is plenty of free on-site parking.

BASIC TOUR

Monday through Friday. Note that children eight and under are not allowed on the tours.

SIDE TRIPS

- **The Giant's Causeway** Walk along the magnificent cliffs on the Yellow Trail or hike down to the beach area to get an ocean-level perspective of these natural wonders.
- **Dunluce Castle** You can walk through the gate and snap some photos of the ruins outside the admissions area, but I can tell you from experience that you will miss some significant history and a tremendous view from inside the ruins.

CLOSEST DISTILLERIES

- **Hinch Distillery** (S-71 mi)
- **Copeland Distillery** (SW-75 mi)

At A Glance

BRAND	Bushmills
WHISKEYS	Single Malt, Blend
FIRST BARREL FILLED	1784
AVAILABLE TO TOUR	Fermenters, Pot Still
TOUR COST	££ — Senior, Student, Child Discounts
WEBSITE	*bushmills.com*
LOCATION	Bushmills BT57 8QT, United Kingdom

Drew's Top Three Reasons to Visit

1 This hour-long tour includes a tasting at a very nice price. If you are just dipping your toe in the world of distillery tours, it is an excellent place to start.

2 During this tour, you get to understand the influence wood has on a whiskey by sticking your nose in ex-bourbon, ex-Oloroso and ex-port-wine barrels.

3 Whiskey Lore podcast fans will already know that the 1608 license to distill was not specific to Bushmills and the current buildings only date to after the great fire of 1885. Still, the history here is palatable, and the distillery is rich with stories and lore.

MORE INFORMATION: *whiskey-lore.com/bushmills*

Copeland Distillery

ABOUT COPELAND DISTILLERY

Great things are happening on the Ard Peninsula east of Belfast. As you make your way to the little seaside town of Donaghadee, it is worth a stop off to visit Copeland Distillery. Grab a coffee or tea in the coffee shop at the very least, or take a tour and learn about the origins of the distillery and the history of the area.

The vision for this distillery came from the mind of Gareth Irvine who, at 22, set out to create his own line of spirits. He started with pink gin, but by 2019 had moved the operations to a larger facility in town and added whiskeys to the lineup. They are currently sourcing their main whiskey brand, Merchant's Quay, but new make is being created with a target date of 2024 for the release. Copeland's Jones 1778 Navy Strength Gin is hard for the whiskey lover to ignore. They age it for 120 days in ex-bourbon barrels, 20 days in Oloroso sherry barrels, and released at 57% ABV—it certainly turned this whiskey lover's head.

This distillery is still a bit of a hidden gem, and tours can be informal. You'll hear the history of nearby Copeland Island and the story of American patriot John Paul Jones. Tastings can include their gin and rum; I had the privilege of tasting their double-distilled chocolate malt, pot still, and peated malts, as well as a corn- and rye-based whiskey. The future of Copeland's Irish whiskey looks bright.

LISTEN/WATCH FOR

There are several myths about Irish whiskey that have developed over the years. One is that all Irish whiskey is smooth and that this is due to it all being triple distilled. Count the pot stills at Copeland and learn if this is fact or lore.

GETTING THERE

With its location in town, near the waterfront, your GPS will probably take you down a couple of one-lane streets. Just take it slow if you are not used to driving in Irish towns. There is parking on-site, but be prepared to make use of metered on-street parking on busier days.

BASIC TOUR

Friday and Saturday

SIDE TRIPS

- **Ulster Folk and Transport museums** Do you have ancestors from this area or do you love diving into an area's culture and history? These two museums provide a great depth of information.
- **Donaghadee Lighthouse** Built in 1836, this was the first electrically lit lighthouse in Ireland. Walk along the wharf for magnificent views. Kids will enjoy the park, and see if you can spot Scotland during a sunset stroll.

CLOSEST DISTILLERIES

- **Echlinville Distillery** (S-14 mi)
- **Hinch Distillery** (SW-23 mi)

At A Glance

BRAND	Copeland's Merchant Quay
WHISKEYS+	Pot Still, Single Malt, Blend, Gin, Rum
FIRST BARREL FILLED	2019
AVAILABLE TO TOUR	Fermenters, Pot Still, Bottling
TOUR COST	£££
WEBSITE	*copelanddistillery.com*
LOCATION	Manor St, Donaghadee BT21 0HF, United Kingdom

Drew's Top Three Reasons to Visit

1 I have my calendar marked for when we get to 2024: this is the year Copeland's expects to release their own distillate as whiskey. The new make is so good now, I can't imagine what it will be like when it has reached maturity.

2 Donaghadee is a great little seaside town to stroll around. You won't believe how close you are to the shores of Scotland. Take a trip up to the historic castle on the hill, enjoy local shops and restaurants, and enjoy the view of the picturesque lighthouse.

3 If you're short on time, hop in for a cup of coffee or tea and hang with the locals in Copeland's on-site café.

MORE INFORMATION: *whiskey-lore.com/copeland*

Echlinville Distillery

ABOUT ECHLINVILLE DISTILLERY

For the fan of whiskey that wants a total experience, Echlinville Distillery is one to keep on your radar. In 2007, Shane and Lynn Braniff purchased the historic Echlinville Estate and Manor House and are using the surrounding farm and buildings to build an amazing farm-to-glass distillery experience. As of 2022, construction continues on an experience that will start with the growing of the barley, include on-site maltings, take you through the distilling process and into a whiskey maturation warehouse, and end with a tasting. And what a tasting it should be.

For those who have tasted Dunville's long-aged Irish whiskeys, this is a sample of what Echlinville is looking to achieve when its own spirits come of age. And since this distillery is family owned, they have the patience to wait for their spirits to mature. In fact, most people don't realize that Echlinville was actually one of the first of the new breed of distilleries back when Teeling and Dingle were getting underway. Echlinville expects their first whiskey to be over ten years old upon its release.

If you are in the area, however, there's no need to wait as they are currently hosting introductory tours. Start with tea or coffee and scones, hear the history of the manor and brands, and use the vouchers they provide to do a tasting or, if you are a driver, use them for discounts on spirits in the gift shop.

LISTEN/WATCH FOR

When you learn about the distilling process at Echlinville, see if they mention distilling potatoes. They are one of the few distilleries in this book that distill spuds. Find out how they use that distillate.

GETTING THERE

Getting into the distillery grounds was a little tricky for me, because there wasn't any signage, though I expect that to be cleared up by the time you visit. The road on the way in is narrow, but there is enough room for two cars; just take it slow. They have a large car park that was built in preparation for the future full-scale tours.

BASIC TOUR

Saturdays (watch for an expanded schedule)

SIDE TRIPS

- **Mount Stewart Estate** Explore the beautiful botanical gardens.
- **Exploris Aquarium** Located in nearby Portaferry, here the kids can enjoy a fun afternoon watching seals, otters, turtles, and crocodiles, while learning about Northern Ireland's sea life.

CLOSEST DISTILLERIES

- **Copeland Distillery** (N-14 mi)
- **Hitch Distillery** (W-27 mi)

At A Glance

BRANDS	Dunville's, Old Comber, Matt D'Arcy, Feckin
WHISKEYS+	Pot Still, Single Malt, Grain, Blend, Poitín, Gin
FIRST BARREL FILLED	2019
AVAILABLE TO TOUR	Milling, Fermenters, Column Still, Pot Stills, Warehouse
TOUR COST	££
WEBSITE	*echlinville.com*
LOCATION	62 Gransha Rd, Kircubbin, Newtownards BT22 1AJ, United Kingdom

Drew's Top Three Reasons to Visit

1 Echlinville is growing to become the most feature-rich distillery experience on the island. As of this writing it is already an entertaining and informative tour, but soon it will include things you rarely see at distilleries, including a view of grain fields, a malting floor, and bottling. Get a chance to see the work in progress and learn about how this family based distillery is taking their time to create incredible whiskeys and a top notch experience.

2 Within one room, view equipment that is versatile enough to create all of Ireland's styles of whiskey. Here they have the flexibility to double distill, triple distill, and to make grain whiskey from a column still.

3 The drive down the Ard Peninsula from Belfast is absolutely beautiful. Come down A20 along Strangford Lough for a beautiful view but be prepared to be slowed by trucks (lorries) along the way. Note too that the on-site Echlinville Manor House may soon offer lodgings, making this an outstanding whiskey destination.

MORE INFORMATION: *whiskey-lore.com/echlinville*

Hinch Distillery

ABOUT HINCH DISTILLERY

At Hinch Distillery, prepare to see a first-generation family distillery with a focus on Irish whiskey's heritage, sustainability, and a farm-to-glass mentality. Dr. Terry Cross has taken his experience of starting a vineyard and, with lessons learned, built a distillery, restaurant, and event space south of Belfast. The result is a well-crafted tour where your guide describes every element of the process.

One of the standout features of this tour is how they incorporate sensory moments. After a short promotional video, the guide lets you smell malted, unmalted, and peated barley. Then, following a review of the milling process, you walk the floor of the distillery and hear a thorough explanation of how they make whiskey. And, even though there isn't a warehouse on-site, you will get a chance to smell the angel's share—and in a very creative way. Hinch also provides one of the most visually complete experiences I've ever seen when it comes to understanding barrel influence.

The guide on my tour was exceptional and welcomed questions. During the tasting, they gave those that may have decided on the smaller tasting package an option to upgrade their tasting right on the spot. This is a well thought out piece of flexibility. Plus, they do tours seven days a week, which makes planning multiple distillery tours easier.

LISTEN/WATCH FOR

Look for the names on each of the stills. Whereas many distilleries will give human names to each of their stills, Hinch uses the name of local mountains. If you are curious, ask your guide about each mountain's name.

GETTING THERE

This is one of the easiest distilleries to get to, located just south of Belfast on the A24. The entrance is clearly marked and there is ample parking on the premises.

BASIC TOUR

Daily

SIDE TRIPS

- **The Titanic Belfast** If Kate and Leo mesmerized you, learn the actual history of the Titanic and watch out for a linked distillery experience coming soon.
- **Carrickfergus Castle** Visit an 800-year-old fortress that has stood the test of time.

CLOSEST DISTILLERIES

- **Rademon Estate Distillery** (SE-9 mi)
- **Copeland Distillery** (NE-23 mi)

At A Glance

BRANDS	Hinch
WHISKEYS+	Pot Still, Single Malt, Blend, Gin
FIRST BARREL FILLED	2017
AVAILABLE TO TOUR	Fermentation, Pot Stills, Bottling
TOUR COST	£££ — Child Discounts
WEBSITE	*hinchdistillery.com*
LOCATION	19 Carryduff Rd, Ballynahinch BT27 6TZ, United Kingdom

Drew's Top Three Reasons to Visit

1 If you are new to Irish whiskey and are looking for a distillery tour that will walk you through the entire process of making whiskey, with bits of Irish history to give context, this is the one to choose.

2 This is the first distillery I've been to where they thoroughly talk through the milling and mashing process, and you get to see your guide demonstrating what water does when mixed with the grist.

3 During the tasting, the guide will walk you through nosing and tasting a whiskey and gives everyone an opportunity to relate their experience. Don't hesitate to share your own experience. We all have different noses, palates, and tasting experiences. There are no right or wrong answers—only subjective experiences.

MORE INFORMATION: *whiskey-lore.com/hinch*

Rademon Estate Distillery

ABOUT RADEMON ESTATE DISTILLERY

If you ask around, you might hear most people refer to Shortcross Gin, rather than whiskey. What they may not realize is David and Fiona Boyd-Armstrong's original passion was to bring craft whiskey distilling back to Northern Ireland. Owners of a historic 500-acre estate and inspired by a book on the lost distilleries of Ireland, the couple traveled the world, learning about the drinks industry, and getting a sense of their homeland's place in it. After learning the art of distilling, they built a distillery and soon their gin took off. Then David dived into creating single malts and his unique malted rye and malted barley mash bill. Always open to experimentation, he also distills a single pot still whiskey and has a peated whiskey in the works as well.

The tour weaves its way inside and outside the distillery. There is a nice balance of history, David and Fiona's journey to building the distillery, a review of the whiskey-making process, and a trip to the warehouse.

With the standard Whiskey Tasting & Tour Experience, they gave me the option to start the tour with a cocktail. At the end of the tour, we enjoyed a guided tasting of poitín and Irish whiskey. They also give guests an opportunity to dip their own bottle and to custom label it. There are some nice photo opportunities outside, but note that photography is discouraged in the still house.

LISTEN/WATCH FOR

How many distilleries can you distinguish from space? Listen during your tour for clues as to what makes this distillery easy to spot from the air.

GETTING THERE

You will probably need GPS to find the location. For Google Maps users, it is advisable to download your maps before you go. Be careful on the winding roads on the way as they are good quality but narrow. When you arrive, you may need to ring for someone at the gate. You'll also need to use caution driving down the single track roads within the estate itself. There are plenty of paved parking spots once you arrive at the distillery.

BASIC TOUR

Fridays and Saturdays.

SIDE TRIPS

- **Inch Abbey** See what remains of this 12th and 13th century Abbey; it's on the north bank of the Quoile River.
- **Ballydugan Medieval Settlement** Learn about culture and the area's heritage while throwing axes and meeting vikings. A great family-based attraction that brings history to life.

CLOSEST DISTILLERIES

- **Hinch Distillery** (NW-9 mi)
- **Copeland Distillery** (NE-26 mi)

At A Glance

BRAND	Shortcross
WHISKEYS+	Pot Still, Single Malt, Grain, Blend, Poitín, Gin
FIRST BARREL FILLED	2015
AVAILABLE TO TOUR	Fermenters, Pot Still, Warehouse
TOUR COST	£££
WEBSITE	*rademonestatedistillery.com*
LOCATION	65 Church Rd, Downpatrick BT30 9HR, United Kingdom

Drew's Top Three Reasons to Visit

1 The tour features the background of Rademon Estate, which dates back to 1667. The 500 acres surrounding the estate and distillery have a history that goes back even further—to A.D.565.

2 Co-founder David Boyd-Armstrong likes to use malted grains, and on the tour, you will taste Shortcross poitín, which is made with malted barley, malted wheat, and malted rye.

3 If you are curious about or are a fan of rye, David has put a lot of focus on the grain, featuring Irish rye in their core Shortcross Rye & Malt Irish Whiskey. It is well worth a try.

MORE INFORMATION: *whiskey-lore.com/shortcross*

NORTHERN IRELAND

Northern Ireland Considerations

AN CARN

This is an early stage project whose website caught my attention when I first started planning my trip around Ireland. It is in the early stages, but the owners are moving forward with plans to build a farm distillery. Located in South Derry, close to Bushmills, the distillery project will focus on sustainability, tradition, and the use of local barley. Estimated opening in 2024. Watch the website for further details.

FEATURED BRAND	TBD
FIRST BARREL FILLED	TBD
TOURS	TBD (check website for updates)
WEBSITE	*ancarndistillery.com*

GLENS OF ANTRIM DISTILLERY

Between Belfast and the Giant's Causeway lies a beautiful coastal road just begging for a whiskey destination. Enter a family of potato farmers and crisp makers, who are looking to diversify into the world of Irish whiskey and bring long overdue attention to their community. The planned distillery will focus on tourism, sustainability, and delivering a taste of the area.

Their current sourced whiskey is called Lír after the fabled story of King Lír and his four children, who were turned into swans. The elegantly crafted bottle should be a sign of things to come. The distillery will focus on triple-distilled single malts and blends, with PX and Oloroso sherry casks being secured for maturation. Beyond the distillery, the plans include a high-quality restaurant, whiskey excursions to Islay and the Scottish peninsula of Kintyre, and to turn the town of Cushendall into a destination rather than a place to pass through on the way up or down the coast. Estimated opening in 2024.

FEATURED BRAND	Lír
WHISKEYS+	Single Malt, Blend, Poitín
FIRST BARREL FILLED	TBD
TOURS	TBD (check website for updates)
WEBSITE	*glensofantrimdistillery.com*

J&J MCCONNELL'S DISTILLERY

Whisky distilling is coming back to Belfast in a big way, with the return of J&J McConnell's. Established as a brand in 1776, this once- great brand survived both fires and a major downturn in Irish whiskey sales. Yet, eventually, it was overwhelmed and had to close. A few years ago, the brand returned to the market with an excellent affordable blend and followed that up with a sherry cask offering. Now there is a distillery being built in Wing A of Belfast's Crumlin Road Gaol. Here, two pieces of history will come together—a legacy whisky brand and a place of incarceration that touched so many lives in Belfast during the Troubles.

These are exciting times in the city, and McConnell's is a continuation of its rebirth. For Irish whiskey fans, this gives you a chance to park yourself in Belfast, where you can both visit distilleries and take in the excellent nightlife that has developed downtown. Watch the website or follow them on social media to find out when they are open for tours.

FEATURED BRAND	McConnell's
WHISKEYS	Blend
FIRST BARREL FILLED	TBD
TOURS	TBD (check website for updates)
WEBSITE	*mcconnellsirishwhisky.com*

KILLOWEN DISTILLERY

When you see something falling short of expectations, you take the bull by the horns. That spirit is in Brendan Carty, a man who realized that Irish whiskey wasn't living up to its history or its potential. He took matters into his own hands and built what he calls his "protest distillery."

If there is something that needs to be tried and sounds like it will push the Irish whiskey industry forward, Brendan will try it. His little white shed distillery up in the hills harkens back to an era when the backcountry was littered with illegal stills crafting poitín and Irish pot still whiskey. Brendan went to Portugal to have his stills custom crafted and kept the focus on creating a clean spirit with as much copper contact as possible. Keeping with the old ways, his stills are fire fed and he incorporates a worm tub to create a more pleasing distillate. He also incorporates the grain that Irish whiskey forgot—oats. And he uses them liberally in his distillations, whether or not it follows the current rules. To Brendan, it is about the spirit, more than the rules.

The small footprint of the distillery makes standardizing tours a little difficult, but Branden says to reach out to him if you want to see it firsthand.

FEATURED BRANDS	Killowen (Bonded Series), Killowen
WHISKEYS+	Pot Still, Blend, Rye, Poitín, Rum, Gin
FIRST BARREL FILLED	2019
TOURS	Ask
WEBSITE	*killowendistillery.com*

LIMAVADY DISTILLERY

Imagine, after a 17 year career at Bushmills, you discover your hometown has a distilling legacy that predates your legendary former employers. What would you do? Well, for Darryl McNally, it was time to head home, join his family, and rediscover that heritage.

His first job was to reintroduce the Limavady name to the Irish whiskey industry. Darryl has done so by sourcing a uniquely flavored single malt that he finishes in Pedro Ximénez casks. He packages this whiskey in a one-of-a-kind bottle that harkens back to a bygone era of hand-blown glass. As of 2022, plans are being completed for a new distillery in Limavady, so this is another one to keep on your radar.

FEATURED BRAND	Limavady
WHISKEYS	Single Malt
TOURS	TBD (check website for updates)
WEBSITE	*limavady.com*

TITANIC DISTILLERS

Fans of the historic ship and the movie *Titanic* have a new whiskey distillery to look forward to. Being built in the old pump house that, for just a brief moment in time, was dwarfed by the great "unsinkable" ship, this is the only authentic landmark related to the doomed vessel (which was built in the city). The pump house is being historically preserved, with the addition of three copper pot stills overlooking the scene. There are also plans for a café, speakeasy, visitor's center, and a tasting room. The tour will embrace the history of distilling, the docks, and the shipyard workers. The distillery plans to open for tours in December 2022.

FEATURED BRAND	Titanic Distillers
WHISKEYS+	Blend, Vodka
FIRST BARREL FILLED	TBD
TOURS	TBD (check website for updates)
WEBSITE	*titanicdistillers.com*

North Wild Atlantic Way Whiskey Distillery Map

1	**ACHILL ISLAND DISTILLERY**	7	BAOILLEACH DISTILLERY
2	**ARDARA DISTILLERY**	8	BURREN DISTILLERY
3	**THE CROLLY DISTILLERY**	9	CONNACHT DISTILLERY
4	**LOUGH MASK DISTILLERY**	10	LOUGH GILL DISTILLERY
5	**MICIL DISTILLERY**	11	NEPHIN DISTILLERY
6	**THE SHED DISTILLERY**		

Achill Island Distillery

ABOUT ACHILL ISLAND DISTILLERY

If you love the idea of family-run distilleries, Achill Island will give you what you are looking for and more. It was founded by John McKay, whose dream was to make IrishAmerican a Prohibition-era themed brand that focused on creating strong bonds between Ireland and the descendents of those who left for America. Their logo embraces this connection by featuring a famine ship in honor of the most famous boat of them all, the *Jeannie Johnson*. Sadly, John passed away, but his children have picked up the mantle and are fulfilling his distillery dreams.

It is possible one of John's two sons, Michael or Sean, will conduct your tour. As they walk you through the history, they will tell you stories of the family, the famine, and the island. The passion for the brand is clear from the moment you walk in. Then they introduce you to how they create both single malt and pot still whiskey on their two Forsyth stills. They emphasize their slow distillation process, which helps create the highest quality spirit possible.

The tour ends in the front bar where you can relax, ask questions, and enjoy samples of whiskey and a locally inspired cocktail. You will also receive a nice polaroid photo to remember your experience by—or you can leave it on the Cowboy Whiskey Wall to keep a lasting connection with the distillery and the family that runs it.

LISTEN/WATCH FOR

Look for green and red around the Scottish pot stills and in the cocktail that is served at the end of the tour. These are in honor of the official colors featured in the flag of County Mayo.

GETTING THERE

Because of its distance, Achill Island works better as a destination. However, I did manage to fit in a couple of distilleries on the day I visited. Getting here involves a decent drive out on regional road R319, but it isn't a difficult trip. Just watch the local roads your GPS may try to send you down on the way to the island. There is a good bit of parking when you arrive.

BASIC TOUR

Thursday through Sunday (seasonal).

SIDE TRIPS

- **Keel Beach** I was told this is one of the most beautiful beaches in the world and that it is best visited on cooler, rainy days as it can get quite busy.
- **Wild Nephin National Park** A hidden gem among Ireland's national parks. Start with the visitors' center and bring snacks if you plan to make a day of it.

CLOSEST DISTILLERIES

- **Lough Mask Distillery** (SE-84 km)
- **Micil Distillery** (SE-141 km)

At A Glance

BRANDS	Achill Island, IrishAmerican
WHISKEYS	Single Malt, Blend
FIRST BARREL FILLED	2019
AVAILABLE TO TOUR	Fermenters, Pot Still, Warehouse
TOUR COST	€€ — Child Discounts
WEBSITE	*irishamericanwhiskeys.com*
LOCATION	Unit 2 udaras na gaeltachta Bunnacurry Achill Island, Westport, Co. Mayo, F28 AY75, Ireland

Drew's Top Three Reasons to Visit

1 Michael and his family are inspirational. The distillery is rich with stories, though not all happy ones. Yet the family has come together, pitched in and they are building the generational business their father dreamed of—connecting Ireland with Americans of Irish descent. It's a heartwarming experience.

2 The distillery's bar is a nice place to unwind at the end of your tour, especially at the end of a long day.

3 Achill Island is a popular getaway for the Irish. There are plenty of natural wonders around, from beaches to national parks. You can visit a deserted 19th-century village or take the kids to the aquarium. The area also hosts its own summer film festival. Plus, you'll find touristy geographical curiosities here, like the westernmost restaurant in Europe and the smallest pub on Achill.

MORE INFORMATION: *whiskey-lore.com/achillisland*

Ardara (Sliabh Liag) Distillery

ABOUT ARDARA DISTILLERY

James and Moira met in Zimbabwe and spent time in Africa in the tea and coffee business. After James worked in the beer and whiskey industries, he came home to Donegal to reclaim the area's true distilling heritage. Far from Dublin, in terms of location and style, what Ardara seeks to produce is much closer to the illicit spirits his grandfather made in the past—and what some in the region still make to this day.

One of the chief characteristics of local poitín and whiskey is its smokiness. This smoke comes from the most prevalent heating source in the area: turf (known to whiskey drinkers as peat). In the days when transportation was limited in these areas, coal could be hard to get, so turf would be used for everything from heating homes to malting grains for spirits. Ardara has gone all in on this historically accurate whiskey-making technique and will bring that smoky character to all of their whiskeys. If you haven't acquired a taste for smoky whiskey, this may be the best place to learn, as their triple distillation seeks to bring a softer character to the whiskey. As you walk through the distillery, enjoy the smoky character mixed with the sweet grain aromas.

Tours take you through the history of the region, the concept of illicit distilling, and will give you a chance to taste multiple expressions through a guided tasting of their gin, sourced whiskey, and potentially some new make, if you request it.

LISTEN/WATCH FOR

There are a lot of subtle differences between how Ardara makes their whiskey versus everyone else. In addition to only making whiskeys with peat, they also distill the grain with the wort. If you visit several distilleries on your trip, see how many differences you can spot in Ardara's process and whiskey.

GETTING THERE

The easiest way to visit the distillery is to find the main car park in the village of Ardara or park on the street. The car park is located just off of N56 on Charlie Bennett Drive. You will see the distillery on the other side of the river; take the walking path into the village, cross the bridge and it's an eight-minute walk down Drumbaran Street onto Donegal Road. The distillery is on the left. The distillery is also providing accessibility parking in front of the distillery.

BASIC TOUR

Monday through Saturday. No children under eight on the tour.

SIDE TRIPS

- **Sliabh Liag Cliffs** Hike or take a bus or van ride from the visitors' center to these magnificent cliffs—the highest accessible in Europe—where stunning views await.
- **Crohy Head Sea Arch** A short drive from the distillery, Arch Stack known as Bristí (or Bristé) highlights a series of fascinating rock formations off the shoreline

CLOSEST DISTILLERIES

- **Crolly Distillery** (N-39 km)
- **The Shed Distillery** (S-110 km)

At A Glance

BRANDS	Ardara, Sliabh Liag, Silkie
WHISKEYS+	Single Malt, Pot Still, Blend, Poitin, Gin
FIRST BARREL FILLED	2020
AVAILABLE TO TOUR	Milling, Fermenters, Pot Still, Warehouse
TOUR COST	€€ — Children eight and over free
WEBSITE	*sliabhliagdistillers.com*
LOCATION	The Show Field, Woodhill, Ardara, Donegal F94 EH7X, Ireland

Drew's Top Three Reasons to Visit

1 If you love smoke and you are an Islay fan, this is a distillery to put on your list— every whiskey is peated. And this is the first distillery I visited that has a triple-distilled, peated, old Irish pot still whiskey in the works.

2 James and Moira embrace the area's history, the history of illicit distilling, and the old single pot still recipes. Something to look forward to is the release of their 1920s pot-still recipe that uses malted and peated oats.

3 Ardara is a festival town and a wonderful jumping off point for exploring Donegal or for a pleasant stop on the journey down the Wild Atlantic Way.

MORE INFORMATION: *whiskey-lore.com/ardara*

Crolly Distillery

ABOUT CROLLY DISTILLERY

Opened in 2022 in a former carpet and doll factory, the Crolly Distillery turns back the clock to celebrate the history of its building, and the people and culture of the area. The hills of the surrounding countryside echo with a long legacy of illegal poitín distillation as the last legal distillery in this area shut its doors over 180 years ago. In 2018, three friends from Crolly decided it was time to bring legal distilling back to the region.

The locals have been raving about the care and attention to detail being put into this project. Though the building has been upgraded, it has retained much of its original character; the distillery reveals its stories through expert tour guides, visuals, and with a selection of local food in the cafe. Locals will feel right at home, while visitors with ancestry in the area will gain a deeper appreciation of their roots.

The distillery tour includes a full review of the whiskey-making process, with visuals to aid your understanding. Then you will walk among the stills and smell the angel's share in the warehouse while you learn about their aging process. At the conclusion of the tour, you'll enjoy a tasting of whiskeys aged in European, Irish, and American oak while getting all of your questions answered. The passion for the area and for whiskey making is clear from the moment you start your tour. It won't be long before the secret is out about this place.

LISTEN/WATCH FOR

In its former life as a carpet factory, the products produced in this building went to a number of famous and infamous customers. See if you can catch who they were.

GETTING THERE

Situated on the Wild Atlantic Way, the distillery is right on the principal thoroughfare for the region, the N56. Flights from Dublin arrive into nearby Donegal Airport, from where you can take a bus into town and to the distillery. There is plenty of on-site parking.

BASIC TOUR

Daily with shorter Wednesday through Sunday schedules in the off-season. Check the website to verify and book your tour.

SIDE TRIPS

- **Boyeeghter Bay, aka Murder Hole Beach** This is one of the most beautiful beaches in Ireland, but has a sense of mystery because of its name.
- **Glenveagh National Park** A jewel of a park filled with spectacular scenery and a castle to visit as well.

CLOSEST DISTILLERIES

- **Ardara Distillery** (S-40 km)
- **Bushmills Distillery** (E-148 km)

At A Glance

BRAND	Croithlí
WHISKEYS	Pot Still, Single Malt
FIRST BARREL FILLED	2020
AVAILABLE TO TOUR	Milling, Fermenters, Cognac Still, Warehouse
TOUR COST	€€ — Family, Child Discounts
WEBSITE	*thecrollydistillery.com*
LOCATION	The Old Doll Factory, Killindarragh, Crolly, Co. Donegal, F92 F7Y3, Ireland

Drew's Top Three Reasons to Visit

1 Here is something you don't see every day at an Irish whiskey distillery: direct flame-fired Cognac stills. Sourced directly from France and refurbished to make whiskey, these stills may be the most beautiful you will see at any distillery in Ireland. They are also just some of the handful that still use a live flame for heat. The brick foundations add even more character to these stunners.

2 If your family came from the area or you have a deep interest in Irish history and culture, this is a great place to start your exploration of the region. The distillery experience gives you a sense of place.

3 Part of the tour focuses on the use of different wood types. Crolly is one of the few distilleries in Ireland that is mixing in Irish oak along with American and European oak. The whiskey goes under the Irish-language brand name Croithlí.

MORE INFORMATION: *whiskey-lore.com/crolly*

Lough Mask (Loch Measc) Distillery

ABOUT LOUGH MASK DISTILLERY

If you are looking for a distillery in a stunning area of the country, look no further than Lough Mask Distillery, or Drioglann Loch Measc as they spell it in the Irish language. Hiding away in the lush green mountains that surround the shores of Lough Mask, this micro-distillery honors the local language and culture.

The tour gives you a sense of the area's distilling past. A historic photo of an illicit distilling operation and its owner providing a tour shows how bold local distillers were in the 19th century. As you walk through the distilling operation, you will learn how they make their double-distilled single malt, as well as their gin and vodka—the gin is infused with a variety of local botanicals. The whiskeys are being aged in European and American oak, with some peated whiskey expected in the future. The pandemic slowed operations, but whiskey production has returned to a consistent level as of 2022.

A highlight of the tour is the view of the fire-fed alembic Portuguese stills that were custom designed and hammered by coppersmiths to resemble their ancient ancestors. Lough Mask adapted the rest of the recycled equipment to fit their needs.

Expect an hour-long tour that is molded to your interests. The tasting at the end includes samples of their gin and vodka, and will soon also include their whiskey.

LISTEN/WATCH FOR

During your tour, you may hear the story of the Hawthorn Tree. Surrounded by water, this defiant tree faces all kinds of weather. They immortalized it in the brand's logo.

GETTING THERE

Whether coming from Donegal or Galway, my best advice for avoiding single-track roads is to enter and exit the area by the R330 and R300, heading south from Partry off the N34. After driving along the Lough for 14 km, bear right down the L5630, where you will find the distillery entrance a short distance up the road. There is plenty of parking. I highly suggest downloading offline maps for smartphone-based GPS.

BASIC TOUR

Monday through Friday

SIDE TRIPS

- **Curraghduff Farm** Walk alpacas, learn about them, and even do some glamping (luxury camping) on this family farm. Reservations are required.
- **Aasleagh Falls** Enjoy a walk to this short but impressive and photogenic waterfall.

CLOSEST DISTILLERIES

- **Micil Distillery** (SE-77 km)
- **Achill Island Distillery** (NW-84 km)

At A Glance

BRAND	Loch Measc
WHISKEYS+	Single Malt, Vodka, Gin
FIRST BARREL FILLED	2022
AVAILABLE TO TOUR	Fermenters, Pot Stills, Warehouse, Bottling
TOUR COST	€€
WEBSITE	*loughmaskdistillery.com*
LOCATION	Tourmakeady, Killateeaun, Co. Mayo, F12 PK75, Ireland

Drew's Top Three Reasons to Visit

1 One of the prettiest drives you will take on an island filled with beautiful landscapes. A view in one direction yields the greenest mountains around; look in the other direction and you'll see more earthy greens and weathered mountains.

2 These are some of the smallest pot stills in Ireland. This is not a distillery about speed. They hope to produce around 100 barrels of whiskey a year.

3 If you are a fan of gin, consider checking out their personalized tours where you can bring your own botanicals and craft your own.

MORE INFORMATION: *whiskey-lore.com/loughmask*

Micil Distillery

ABOUT MICIL DISTILLERY

It is amazing to think that a town as big as Galway, in a whiskey-loving country like Ireland, hadn't seen a whiskey distillery in a century. But thanks to Micil Distillery, all of that has now changed. The distillery was named in honor of the founder's great-great-great-grandfather, Micil Mac Chearra, who distilled illicit poitín in the hills of Connemara over 170 years ago. The tradition passed down through six generations, and today Pádraic and Jimín Ō Griallais are breaking new ground by distilling legally under a license.

With all of that rich tradition behind them, there are plenty of stories of illicit distilling during the tour. The distillery's small footprint means that there isn't a lot of walking on this tour: in fact, the distillery equipment is located downstairs, so you get a bird's-eye view of the distillation process. From the comfort of the bar area, you will have multiple chances to taste whiskey and poitín while enjoying a guided tasting and an opportunity to chat with your tour mates.

While Micil's in-house spirits wait for the day they officially become Irish whiskey, Earls Island Single Pot Still Whiskey gives you a preview of things to come. Finished in ex-Bordeaux and peated casks, the flavors hark back to the days when Galway was a great trading port with France and Spain. The future release of Micil's Heritage Pot Still goes beyond current rules to help you rediscover historic flavors of old Irish pot still whiskey.

LISTEN/WATCH FOR

This is a distillery that embraces its Irish heritage. When you walk in, you will see the brand's logo and namesake holding a bushel of barley. You will also see the words *Fuisce Mhicil* and find out what this means, and also discover how they pronounce poitín.

GETTING THERE

Parking isn't difficult as there is plenty of it up along the waterfront, but finding the distillery itself can be a little tricky. You will need to enter through the back of the Oslo Bar and Micro-Brewery. If you're looking to spend some time in Galway, the surrounding Sandhill district is a great section of town, with a beach and plenty of restaurants and cafés.

BASIC TOUR

Tuesday through Saturday

SIDE TRIPS

- **Connemara National Park** After learning about a family (and their spirits) from Connemara, check out their homeland in this playland of bogs, hilltops, hiking, and incredible scenery.
- **Cliffs of Moher Visitor Center** Enjoy a day viewing the birds and wildlife along the cliffs featured in the film *The Princess Bride*. It is an unforgettable view.

CLOSEST DISTILLERIES

- **Lough Mask Distillery** (NW-77 km)
- **Tullamore DEW** (E-115 km)

At A Glance

BRAND	Micil
WHISKEYS+	Pot Still, Poitín, Blend, Gin
FIRST BARREL FILLED	2020
AVAILABLE TO TOUR	Fermenters, Pot Still
TOUR COST	€€€
WEBSITE	*micildistillery.com*
LOCATION	Oslo Bar, 226 Upper Salthill Rd, Galway, H91 N9WK, Ireland

Drew's Top Three Reasons to Visit

1 As I understand it, Pádraic is the primary guide and he is a wonderful storyteller. In fact, I enjoyed his stories so much that I had him on as a guest on my Whiskey Lore: The Interviews podcast. He has a genuine passion for introducing people to Ireland's native spirits and its history.

2 If you are a fan of speakeasies, you will like how you enter the distillery. You first have to make your way through the Oslo Bar, then use the backdoor to find Micil's front door.

3 You might think a distillery so rich in history would stick to the old ways, but look for a lot of innovation from Micil, such as the use of non-standard types of barrels including chestnut, and a variety of different mash bills.

MORE INFORMATION: *whiskey-lore.com/micil*

The Shed Distillery

ABOUT THE SHED DISTILLERY

Be ready to be entertained. Out in the heartland of Ireland, the town of Drumshanbo has become the staging point for an adventure deep into the "creative mind" of world traveler P.J. Rigney. His dream was to find a unique location, rich with stories, where he could distill his Irish whiskey. But he also wanted to create an Irish gin using botanicals found during his many journeys across the globe.

The Shed Distillery is one of the few in Ireland that has been around long enough to have its own in-house whiskey on the market. It was the first whiskey distilled in Connacht in 101 years and P.J. saw no need to rush the release, waiting five years to make sure it was right. In the meantime, the distillery gained fame for its Drumshanbo Gunpowder Irish Gin.

I have never met P.J., but his distillery tour gives the distinct impression that he enjoys a good show with its almost theatrical presentation, and the feeling of adventure permeates this informative tour. After learning about the distilling process and seeing the stills, your guided tasting takes you on a journey of smells and tastes. From there, you jump into the gin-making process while learning about P.J.'s travels. After learning about and smelling some of the botanicals used in Drumshanbo Gunpowder Gin, the tour concludes with a gin cocktail in the bar.

LISTEN/WATCH FOR

The whiskey brand Drumshanbo is often mispronounced and misspelled; in fact, a sign at the old train station in town also misspelled the name. You will get a chuckle when you find out the meaning of the misspelled word versus the proper spelling.

GETTING THERE

Drumshanbo might seem a little isolated, but if you are heading to Donegal or Achill Island from Dublin, or other points east, it is easy to put the distillery in your path. There is ample and easily accessible parking. Just make sure you set your GPS if you are unfamiliar with the area.

BASIC TOUR

Daily

SIDE TRIPS

- **Shannon Blueway Drumshanbo Trailhead** Enjoy the great outdoors with canoeing, biking, and hiking along the Blueway trails, or walk the floating boardwalk.
- **Carrig Brewing Company** For a change of pace, check out this family-run craft brewery and tap room.

CLOSEST DISTILLERIES

- **Kilbeggan Distillery** (S-101 km)
- **Tullamore D.E.W.** (S-114 km)

At A Glance

BRAND	Drumshanbo
WHISKEYS+	Pot Still, Vodka, Gin
FIRST BARREL FILLED	2020
AVAILABLE TO TOUR	Fermenters, Pot Still
TOUR COST	€€ — Senior, Student, Child Discounts
WEBSITE	*thesheddistillery.com*
LOCATION	Carricknabrack, Drumshanbo, Co. Leitrim, N41 R6D7, Ireland

Drew's Top Three Reasons to Visit

1 This is the perfect tour for those who love gin or whiskey, or both. It gives equal time to each and makes discovering both spirits fun and entertaining.

2 The tour includes two tasting opportunities. First, you will experience a guided tasting of Drumshanbo Single Pot Still Irish Whiskey. Then, after seeing and smelling the botanicals, they invite you into the cocktail bar for a chance to sample the gin.

3 Because this tour is daily, it helps those planning an extended distillery adventure across the country, enabling you to visit on days when other distilleries are closed.

MORE INFORMATION: *whiskey-lore.com/shed*

NORTH WILD ATLANTIC WAY

North Wild Atlantic Way Considerations

BAOILLEACH DISTILLERY

Away from it all, in Donegal, stands a small farm distillery. Its owner, Michael O'Boyle, leans heavily on the distilling techniques of an area steeped in tradition, while finding creative ways to move his spirits forward. Using a four-column hybrid still, he is looking beyond triple distillation to create a full-bodied spirit. But he also seeks to be more refined than double-distilled spirits. His focus will be on peated whiskey, with Donegal turf at its core. He stays local by making his poitín with a mixture of Donegal barley and potatoes.

Michael's mantra is "fly your own flag." His inspiration comes from the can-do spirit of American craft distillers and he has worked to incorporate some of those techniques into his spirits as well.

While the distillery isn't the easiest to access, the view of his farm and the surrounding lands makes it well worth the trip. And seeing someone malt their own grains is also a rarity. There is a potential for tours and experiences in the future, so check out the distillery website or reach out to Michael directly.

BRAND	Mulroy Bay
WHISKEYS+	Pot Still, Single Malt, Blend, Poitín, Rum, Gin
FIRST BARREL FILLED	2022
TOURS	Ask
WEBSITE	*baoilleachdistillery.ie*

BURREN DISTILLERY

I can't think of a distiller more passionate about Irish whiskey history, especially when it relates to his own region, than Noel O'Lochlainn. During my visit, I received a detailed history of the region and early Irish Brehon law and traditions. With a distilling heritage going back centuries, Noel seeks to bring that old world into the new. This was one of the few distilleries I visited in Ireland where I saw floor maltings in progress. The grains Noel uses are based on what he has available, just like the farmer-distillers of old. But more than anything, in Noel I see an educator at heart. In fact, while I was there, students were visiting from France and were learning and pitching in on the process.

At the time of writing, there is no brand yet on the market. Distilling started in 2019, and it feels like the focus is more on creating whiskey and honing the craft than marketing a whiskey brand. There isn't a formalized tour at the moment, but if you do ever visit, I promise it will be hard to leave without a bit of Noel's passion in your soul.

BRAND	TBD
WHISKEYS	Single Malt
FIRST BARREL FILLED	2019
TOURS	Ask
WEBSITE	*burrendistillers.com*

CONNACHT DISTILLERY

If you pass a sign that says "Salmon Capital of Ireland" as you drive through County Mayo, you will have reached Ballina, the home of Connacht Distillery. Built in a former bakery, the distillery has several North American ties, from its master distiller Robert Cassell's of New Liberty Distillery in Philadelphia, to its American head distiller Ryan, and its three copper pot stills that come from British Columbia, Canada. Looking to highlight authentic Irish whiskey styles, at the time of my visit they were offering a taste of their traditional Irish poitín made with malted barley, the blended whiskey Ballyhoo, and their first in-house single malt, Connacht Batch 1.

If you would like to taste their spirits, pre-book one of their two tasting time slots at 1 PM or 3 PM, Tuesday through Friday. Tours are limited but available by request and molded to fit each group's interests and experience. Drivers receive a discount.

BRANDS	Ballyhoo, Connacht, Spade & Bushel
WHISKEYS+	Single Malt, Grain, Blend, Poitín, Vodka, Gin
FIRST BARREL FILLED	2016
TOURS	Ask
WEBSITE	*connachtwhiskey.com*

LOUGH GILL DISTILLERY

This is one of the Irish distilleries I have had my eye on for quite some time. The elegant marketing of their brand Athrú raised my curiosity level. When I found out the master of distillery resurrections, Scotland's Billy Walker, was involved in barrel picks and advising on the new make, my curiosity went to a whole new level. With the acquisition of the distillery by Sazerac, the company behind the incredible success of Buffalo Trace, this is a distillery to watch.

A visit to Lough Gill today requires a bit of imagination. The outside of this 1960s former textile and VHS tape factory looks like a relic of that era. Meanwhile, the mansion next door is at the beginning of a major renovation. It is hard to say how long it will be before these are ready for visitors—but a visitors' experience is definitely in the works. The inside of the distillery is spacious and filled with room for growth. Fans of sustainability will appreciate the recycling of energy designed into the system. For the visitor, the layout will create an "oh wow" moment during the first glimpse of the pot stills with the mansion in the windows behind it. From the mansion, there is already an "oh wow" moment, as you look out at the beautiful lands that surround.

There won't be any teasers here about what the tour might be like. It is hard to know at this early stage, but with some imagination, and the knowledge of the company behind them, it's easy to envision something special is coming.

FEATURED BRANDS	Athrú, Paddy's, Michael Collins
WHISKEYS	Single Malt, Blend
FIRST BARREL FILLED	2020
TOURS	TBD (check website for updates)
WEBSITE	*athru.com*

NEPHIN DISTILLERY

Standing in the shadow of the tallest standalone mountain in Ireland, and bearing its name, the Nephin Distillery project is an exciting one. There is so much in the works that will make this distillery stand out, from a possible on-site cooperage to floor maltings, to a focus on energy independence. And following the traditions of this region, it would be one of only two distilleries in the country 100% devoted to making smoky whiskey.

The equipment is there, the building is ready, and the story is waiting to be written. This is a rural distillery that will require GPS to reach. Remember to download maps if you're using Google Maps. The road to the distillery narrows at points so just be careful. The distillery is visible from the road.

FEATURED BRAND	The Cooper
WHISKEY	Single Malt
FIRST BARREL FILLED	TBD
TOURS	TBD (check website for updates)
WEBSITE	*nephinwhiskey.ie*

The South Whiskey Distillery Map

1   BALLYKEEFE DISTILLERY
2   BLACKWATER DISTILLERY
3   CLONAKILTY DISTILLERY
4   DINGLE DISTILLERY
5   KILLARNEY BREWING & DISTILLING
6   MIDLETON DISTILLERY
7   SKELLIG SIX18 DISTILLERY
8   WATERFORD DISTILLERY

9   BLACK'S OF KINSALE DISTILLERY
10 KILLARNEY DISTILLERY
11 ROYAL OAK DISTILLERY
12 TIPPERARY DISTILLERY
13 WAYWARD IRISH SPIRITS
14 WEST CORK DISTILLERY

Ballykeefe Distillery

ABOUT BALLYKEEFE DISTILLERY

If you are a fan of farm distilleries and sustainability, Ballykeefe is one of your best options in Ireland. This is a real working farm with the Ging family managing both the land and the stills. As beef and tillage farmers, they feed their own ecosystem, so there is no waste, and nothing from the whiskey making process leaves the grounds.

Having the owner and distiller take you on your tour is definitely a unique experience. Rather than being given a formulaic tour by a third party, here you can ask questions of the producer and founder. When Morgan Ging shares his whiskey with you during the tasting, he will reveal to you what he seeks to achieve with each expression. He also shares his interest in carrying on the historical traditions of Irish whiskey.

There is no sourcing here. The words "single estate" mean that they grow, harvest, and distill everything on the farm. Their line of triple distilled super-premium single pot still, single malt, and single rye whiskeys use only the hearts of the spirit run, the heads and tails cuts are discarded. They also distill award winning Irish gin, vodka, and poitín.

LISTEN/WATCH FOR

Listen for the story of Ellen Cuffe, Countess of Desart. She took an inheritance and worked to change the course of Irish history. The distillery and farm are part of her former estate and Lady Desart Gin was created to celebrate her legacy.

GETTING THERE

Southwest of Kilkenny, you will drive rural roads through farmland to reach the distillery, so downloading maps in advance is a wise idea. The roads are good and the distillery has plenty of parking out front.

BASIC TOUR

Since this is a working farm, and the distiller normally gives the tours, it is best to contact them through their website for an appointment. Pre-Covid, tours ran in the afternoons five days a week.

SIDE TRIPS

- **Kells Priory** Just the drive to this area alone will give you a genuine sense of the beauty and history of Ireland, and these impressive monastic ruins are well worth exploring.
- **Rock of Cashel** Once the seat of kings, with history that goes back to the time of St. Patrick. The views are incredible from both the hilltop and below. There are plenty of stories and photo opportunities at this impressive structure.

CLOSEST DISTILLERIES

- **Waterford Distillery** (S-53 km)
- **Blackwater Distillery** (SW-95 km)

At A Glance

BRAND	Ballykeefe
WHISKEYS+	Pot Still, Single Malt, Rye, Oat, Poitín, Gin, Vodka
FIRST BARREL FILLED	2017
AVAILABLE TO TOUR	Fermenters, Pot Still, Warehouse, Bottling
TOUR COST	€€€
WEBSITE	*ballykeefedistillery.ie*
LOCATION	Kilballykeefe, Cuffesgrange, Co. Kilkenny, R95 NR50, Ireland

Drew's Top Three Reasons to Visit

1 There are a lot of distilleries that talk about being farm to glass, but here it is clearly visible. At Ballykeefe, a farm surrounds you, and you even get a greeting from cows as you walk from your car to the distillery.

2 A lot of experimentation goes on at Ballykeefe. Morgan has used a variety of grains, and has even distilled 100% malted rye and 100% malted oats.

3 What draws me to this distillery and its whiskey is Morgan's desire to seek the flavors that once made old Irish pure pot still whiskey the most popular in the world.

MORE INFORMATION: *whiskey-lore.com/ballykeefe*

Blackwater Distillery

ABOUT BLACKWATER DISTILLERY

When you have a passion, making money isn't always the first thing on your mind. Author and founder Peter Mulryan has just that kind of focus. A lover of Irish whisky and its history, he set out to build a distillery that could capture the essence of what the spirit was in the past and what it should be now. Appreciative of his neighbor Irish Distillers, Ltd. and how they helped bring Irish whisky back to a world audience, he now wants to push beyond the style they forged in the 1970s and challenge people's understanding of what Irish whisky is.

Following the tradition of whiskey bonders, the distillery's first release revives the historic brand Velvet Cap using sourced whisky. As the in-house Dirtgrain whisky reaches maturity, tastings will shift from sourced whisky and new make to tasting the whiskey they make on-site using 100% Irish grains. You will hear a lot about mash bills as John Wilcox, the head distiller, believes grain choice is crucial to making great whisky.

The tour will provide plenty of history, as Peter has deeply researched Irish whiskey's past. You will also get to meet the author and head distiller during an introductory video. But don't be surprised if you see them on the tour—this is a working distillery after all. After hearing the history and process, you will finish your tour with a Blackwater gin and tonic or a whisky and mixer. There are also opportunities for extended tours, including gin and tonic, and cocktail masterclasses.

LISTEN/WATCH FOR

Blackwater and Boann are both actively recreating several historic old Irish pure pot still mash bills. Listen for what makes these mash bills different from what the current technical file allows. And see if you can catch which little-used grain had a more prominent role in those historic mash bills.

GETTING THERE

The distillery is in an old 1950s hardware store just off R666 in Ballyduff, Co. Waterford. You will find ample parking spots along the street.

BASIC TOUR

Monday, Wednesday, Friday (reservations required).

SIDE TRIPS

- **Cahir Castle** Take a relaxing self-guided tour through a 15th-century castle and gardens. See cannonballs still embedded in the walls, a murder hole, and get your photo taken at the site used for several movies, including the classic *Excalibur*.
- **Father Mathew Statue (Cork)** See the statue of a man who wielded enough power to convert three million Irish citizens into non-drinkers during his famous temperance campaigns.

CLOSEST DISTILLERIES

- **Old Midleton Distillery** (SW-34 km)
- **Waterford Distillery** (E-78 km)

At A Glance

BRANDS	Dirtgrain, Velvet Cap
WHISKEYS+	Pot Still, Single Malt, Blend, Gin, Vodka
FIRST BARREL FILLED	2019
AVAILABLE TO TOUR	Fermenters, Pot Still
TOUR COST	€€
WEBSITE	*blackwaterdistillery.ie*
LOCATION	Church Rd, Ballinlevane East, Ballyduff, Co. Waterford, P51 C5C6, Ireland

Drew's Top Three Reasons to Visit

1 American distiller John Wilcox has embraced the whiskies of Ireland's past and is working on some exciting recreations for future generations to enjoy.

2 It is great to see distilleries working together. Recently Blackwater teamed up with Killowen in Northern Ireland to create the same whisky using the same grains, yeast, and double distillation. The concept was to see how different the spirit would be between two different regions of the island. It helps distillers learn more about the impact of equipment and locations on a whisky.

3 Talk about putting your money where your mouth is. Founder Peter Mulryan spent years as a television producer and author, focusing on the drinks industry. He has channeled that knowledge and passion by putting them into his own spirits.

MORE INFORMATION: *whiskey-lore.com/blackwater*

Clonakilty Distillery

ABOUT CLONAKILTY DISTILLERY

Whether you are starting or ending a trek along the Wild Atlantic Way, a great stopping off point is the town of Clonakilty. And while you are in town, there is a friendly and welcoming distillery waiting for you to visit. Here, not only will you get a foothold on the history and tastes of the region, but you will also enjoy Clonakilty Distillery's award-winning hospitality. Everyone from the tour guides to the distillers are happy and willing to answer questions about the distillery, the town, and their Irish whiskey.

Though the distillery is situated in town, the inspiration for it actually came from the Scully family's 320-year-old farm. Nestled on the south coast near Galley Head Lighthouse, the farm grows a heritage barley not seen in Ireland for over a century. While an amazing grain, its low yields drove accountants crazy, causing it to eventually disappear. Using a sample from the archives, Clonakilty has nurtured and grown enough grain to supply their future in-house distilled pot still and single malt whiskeys.

While the standard tour doesn't include a trip down to the farm, you will get to see it in the introductory video—and don't hesitate to ask how to get there, so you can see it for yourself. At the distillery, enjoy viewing the handmade Italian pot stills and taste their latest releases, and if you love gin, check out their on-site gin school.

LISTEN/WATCH FOR

The reason I am a fan of letting a distillery choose the proof of my whiskey is because I trust them to make the right decision on alcohol strength. Clonakilty opened my eyes to another reason why a distillery can create an advantage in cutting your whiskey for you: keep your ears peeled for details about their "gentle cut" and how it stops the suffocation of your whiskey.

GETTING THERE

There is plenty of on-street parking in the area. If you prefer, there is a large car park a couple of blocks west of the distillery.

BASIC TOUR

April to September: daily; October to March: Wednesday through Sunday

SIDE TRIPS

- **Michael Collins Museum Centre** West Cork is where the Irish independence leader was born and raised, and where he died. This is an excellent place to get a deeper understanding of the man and his times.
- **Galley Head Lighthouse** Get a stunning view of the Atlantic Ocean while you drive past the fields that will provide grain for future bottles of Clonakilty Irish whiskey.

CLOSEST DISTILLERIES

- **Old Midleton Distillery** (NE-74 km)
- **Killarney Brewing & Distilling** (NW-96 km)

At A Glance

BRAND	Clonakilty
WHISKEYS+	Pot Still, Single Malt, Grain, Blend, Gin
FIRST BARREL FILLED	2019
AVAILABLE TO TOUR	Fermenters, Column Still, Pot Still
TOUR COST	€€ — Student, Child Discounts
WEBSITE	*clonakiltydistillery.ie*
LOCATION	The Waterfront, Scartagh, Clonakilty, Co. Cork, P85 N403, Ireland

Drew's Top Three Reasons to Visit

1   This is a great tour—in fact, Ewan Paterson won the visitor attraction manager of the *year* in the Icons of Whisky Awards 2022. The staff are friendly and great to chat with.

2   I am looking forward to tasting their whiskey as it matures. The warehouse is on a peninsula surrounded by the sea, so it will be fun to see how much influence that has on the spirit.

3   Clonakilty is a great town to walk around. Park and enjoy the sights, get lunch or dinner, and learn about Michael Collins and Irish independence—you can get a photo by his statue downtown.

MORE INFORMATION: *whiskey-lore.com/clonakilty*

Dingle Distillery

ABOUT DINGLE DISTILLERY

In deciding which distilleries to give full profiles to, I wanted to keep the two-page profiles to those distilleries with active tours. Having toured and thoroughly enjoyed the Dingle Distillery tour in 2019, I was eager to re-experience it on this trip, in order to include the current experience for your consideration. However, a distillery expansion project and items out of their control have caused a delay in the reopening of their visitors' experience. Thus, it will be 2024 before the distillery reopens to visitors. Still, this is a fantastic tour in a great tourist town, so it should remain on your radar.

The history of Dingle Distillery goes all the way back to the very origins of the Irish whiskey craft revolution. And to prove that, in 2022, they will be the first distillery outside of Cooley, Bushmills, and Midleton to release their own 10-year-old Irish single malt. The distillery features three copper pot stills, a gin still, and a vodka still. You may have seen their younger batch series in the past, but they recently established their blue label single malt as their flagship. They age this whiskey around seven years.

If you are heading to Dingle, keep this distillery in mind. If they haven't opened to tours yet, check to see if there are any tasting experiences in town. Dingle is my favorite town in Ireland, so I don't think a trip there will disappoint you, even if the distillery hasn't quite opened yet.

LISTEN/WATCH FOR

When upgrading the distillery, they wanted to stay consistent with the past and add new wooden mash tuns and fermenters to match their older ones. The only other distillery on the island with this combination is the historic Kilbeggan Distillery.

GETTING THERE

I'm not sure yet what the parking situation will be around the distillery, but there is plenty of parking in the town of Dingle and the walk to the distillery is pleasant, although there is one spot where you may have to walk in the street for a short distance. By parking in town, you can enjoy your tour and not have to worry about driving.

BASIC TOUR

TBD (check website for updates)

SIDE TRIPS

- **Slea Head Drive** This amazing drive to the west of Dingle is a hidden gem, featuring magnificent views, the Valtry Village, the Beehive Hut (Tóchar Maothaithe), and more. Be aware that the road gets narrow in places.
- **Curran's Pub** Dick Mack's is the pub most people will recommend, but I love finding a pub where the locals go. Enjoy a fantastic pour of Guinness here.

CLOSEST DISTILLERIES

- **Killarney Brewing & Distilling** (W-60 km)
- **Skellig Six18 Distillery** (S-96 km)

At A Glance

BRAND	Dingle
WHISKEYS+	Pot Still, Single Malt, Gin
FIRST BARREL FILLED	2012
AVAILABLE TO TOUR	Fermenters, Pot Still, Hybrid Still
TOUR COST	€€
WEBSITE	*dingledistillery.ie*
LOCATION	Farranredmond, Dingle, Co. Kerry, V92 E7YD, Ireland

Drew's Top Three Reasons to Visit

1 My visit to this distillery in 2019 happened right before I went to some 20 scotch distilleries; Dingle rivals many of those distilleries with its polished experience. I really enjoyed the extra insights added during the tour and the friendliness of the guide—I'm bad with names but I still remember my guide's name, which goes to show how impressive they were.

2 This is a great opportunity to taste what time in a cask will do to modern-day Irish craft whiskey.

3 The town of Dingle is a great destination and one where you can easily spend more than a day and night.

MORE INFORMATION: *whiskey-lore.com/dingle*

Killarney Brewing & Distilling Company

ABOUT KILLARNEY BREWING & DISTILLING COMPANY

One of the most amazing places to visit in Ireland is County Kerry, though distilling has been absent from the area for the longest time. That is changing in a major way with the 2023 addition of the Killarney Brewing & Distilling Company's new distillery. Founded by three friends—Tim O'Donoghue, Paul Sheahan, and their Chicago-based business partner, Liam Healy— as a brewery, they have upped the ante by bringing distilling on board and building a state-of-the-art visitors' experience west of town.

Using recycled materials, stone from nearby Valentia Island, and Chicago brick and stone, the founders have spared no expense in developing a drink-lover's paradise. In addition to housing a whiskey distillery, gin distillery and brewery, the building also features a sizable café, 250-seat event space, chocolate shop, and rooftop garden overlooking the lake and mountains.

A look inside the distillery reveals modern equipment including uniquely designed column stills, mash tuns, fermenters, one of only two mash filters in Ireland, and three gorgeous Italian copper pot stills. It will be some time before the spirits from these stills become whiskey. In the meantime, an eight-year-old premium sourced whiskey is being sold under the Killarney name. Watch for the development of a gin school and integration of local grains in their distillate. Look for various tasting options, beer tours, whiskey tours, and a combination of both.

LISTEN/WATCH FOR

After the Great Chicago Fire, the city rebuilt using brick. With the tie-ins to Chicago, the founders sourced Chicago green bricks to use in construction. See if you can spot them when you enter the visitor's center.

GETTING THERE

The distillery is easily accessible with ample parking and is hard to miss on the north side of N72; it's well placed if you're planning to drive the Ring of Kerry or visit Killarney. Local buses and transportation will likely have this as one of their regular stops.

BASIC TOUR

Wednesday through Sunday (subject to change)

SIDE TRIPS

- **Irish Whiskey Experience** After learning about Irish whiskey, head to a place where you can blend, pair, and draw whiskey out of a cask.
- **Muckross House and Abbey** Take a tour of the farm, see the mansion, and walk through the ruins and graveyard of the old abbey.

CLOSEST DISTILLERIES

- **Dingle Distillery** (W-60 km)
- **Skellig Six18 Distillery** (W-56 km)

At A Glance

BRAND	Killarney
WHISKEYS+	Blended, Pot Still, Single Malt, Grain, Gin
FIRST BARREL FILLED	2022
AVAILABLE TO TOUR	Milling, Fermenters, Column Still, Pot Stills, Warehouse, Bottling
TOUR COST	TBD
WEBSITE	*killarneydistilling.com*
LOCATION	Killalee, Killarney, Co. Kerry, V93 FA43, Ireland

Drew's Top Three Reasons to Visit

1 Ever since Aeneas Coffey invented them almost 200 years ago, the column still has always stood out for its ability to create massive amounts of alcohol. Yet, next to its copper pot still cousin, columns are rarely attractive. That all changes with Killarney Distilling. Split into pieces and using a fascinating piping arrangement, I almost spent as much time inspecting the column stills as I did gazing at the beautiful copper pots in front of them.

2 The team here has really done their research. Many of the finer elements and processes used in other Irish distilleries are on display in this one location. This is destined to be another distillery people will reference when you ask, "if I only had time for one distillery visit in Ireland, which would you choose?"

3 If you have an interest in both brewing and distilling, you could easily spend an afternoon here.

MORE INFORMATION: *whiskey-lore.com/killarneybrewing*

Midleton Distillery

ABOUT MIDLETON DISTILLERY

Since the 1970s, the brand that most likely came to mind for Irish whiskey was Jameson. The entire industry owes a debt of gratitude to this distillery, the brand's home, and its owners Pernod-Ricard for keeping the spirit of Irish whiskey alive through some difficult times. Unsurprisingly, given the impact the Jameson brand has had on Irish distilling, this is a very popular tourist destination. Add to that heritage the rebirth of Redbreast, the growth of the Spots, and the birth of the Method and Madness series and the legend continues to grow.

There are several options available if you want to visit the distillery. You can take the standard tour and enjoy a tipple upon its completion; you can dig deeper into the inner workings of distillation and the art of the cooper with a behind-the-scenes tour; or you can extend your tasting experience as your guide takes you through top-notch premium whiskeys. All tours go through the historic Old Midleton Distillery and give you a view of the micro-distillery where Method and Madness was born. Unfortunately, the larger modern distillery is not part of the journey.

Depending on your tour, you may end up in the tasting bar where you can upgrade your tasting or, if you've opted for behind-the-scenes, you will get a special tasting in the Distiller's Cottage and archive building.

LISTEN/WATCH FOR

Because Jameson was so highly promoted and widely available, many of the characteristics we relate to Irish whiskey are thanks to Jameson's extensive marketing efforts. See how many stereotypical terms like 'triple distillation' and 'smooth' you hear during your tour.

Note: If you do the distillery's comparison tasting of scotch, Irish, and American whiskeys, take it with a grain of salt—no country's whiskey should be judged by one brand alone.

GETTING THERE

There is a good amount of parking, but on busy days the spaces can fill up quickly. Leave some extra time to find street parking around town.

BASIC TOUR

Daily

SIDE TRIPS

- **Kindred Spirits: Choctaw Native American Monument** This touching monument celebrates the donation of corn by the North American Choctaw Nation during the Great Potato Famine of the 1840s.
- **Blarney Castle** Kiss the Blarney Stone to get the gift of gab (results may vary) and visit the fascinating poison garden at this legendary castle.

CLOSEST DISTILLERIES

- **Blackwater Distillery** (NE-34 km)
- **Clonakilty Distillery** (SW-76 km)

At A Glance

BRANDS	Jameson, Redbreast, Powers, Method and Madness, The Spots, Midleton
WHISKEYS+	Pot Still, Single Malt, Grain, Blend
FIRST BARREL FILLED	1825
AVAILABLE TO TOUR	Fermenters, Pot Still, Cooperage
TOUR COST	€€ — Senior, Student, Child Discounts
WEBSITE	*jamesonwhiskey.com*
LOCATION	Distillery Walk, Midleton, Co. Cork, P25 Y394, Ireland

Drew's Top Three Reasons to Visit

1 See the 1825 pot still that was once the world's largest in operation. It is an incredible sight to see— it's so big that the room had to be built around it.

2 When you consider that the modern distillery here distilled just about every drop of what was called Irish whiskey in the 1970s and 1980s, it's hard not to want to learn the history they share here.

3 Honestly, as much as I love whiskey history, I had to do the behind-the-scenes tour. Here you get some upgraded tastings, along with a visit to the cooperage, and a premium taste within the Distiller's Cottage.

MORE INFORMATION: *whiskey-lore.com/midleton*

Skellig Six18 Distillery

ABOUT SKELLIG SIX18 DISTILLERY

What do you do with an old Wilson's sock factory? You turn it into a distillery—what else? Named after the iconic Skellig Michael (famously used in *Star Wars: The Force Awakens* as the hideaway for Luke Skywalker) and its hilltop monastery, this gin and whiskey distillery will soon be a regular stop for travelers taking in the world famous Ring of Kerry.

Whiskey production started in 2022. Plans are in place to distill single pot still whiskey using port and sherry casks, like the ones that have been traveling between this area and the European continent for centuries. The distillery has fought the urge to ship in sourced whiskey while they wait for their spirits to age, so tastings will include samples of their gin, which is infused with local botanicals.

The tour will focus on the history of the Ring of Kerry, the town of Cahersiveen, and Skellig Michael. You will also learn about the specifics of whiskey and gin distillation, the use of different woods in the aging process, and how they sourced their botanicals for the gin.

LISTEN/WATCH FOR

This distillery has a unique name. Find out what the Six18 stands for and learn more about the iconic landmark that inspired it.

GETTING THERE

If you're driving the Ring of Kerry, it's right on the main road. There is plenty of parking on-site.

BASIC TOUR

Daily. Children under eight are not allowed on the tour.

SIDE TRIPS

- **Skellig Michael & Mainistir Fhionáin** Charter your boat and get on your hiking shoes to visit the ancient island monastery, one of only two UNESCO World Heritage Sites in Ireland.
- **Kerry Cliffs** Don't shy away from visiting this incredible destination spot on the Wild Atlantic Way and soaking in its incredible view. Bring binoculars to take in a view of Skellig Michael from a distance.

CLOSEST DISTILLERIES

- **Killarney Brewing & Distilling** (E-56 km)
- **Dingle Distillery** (N-96 km)

At A Glance

BRAND	Skellig Six
WHISKEYS+	Single Pot Still, Gin
FIRST BARREL FILLED	TBD
AVAILABLE TO TOUR	Fermenters, Pot Still
TOUR COST	€€ — Senior, Student, Child Discounts
WEBSITE	*skelligsix18distillery.ie*
LOCATION	Valentia Rd, Garranearagh, Cahersiveen, Co. Kerry, V23 YD89, Ireland

Drew's Top Three Reasons to Visit

1 The Ring of Kerry is one of the most beautiful drives in the world. Take a break from the marvelous views to enjoy a gin and whiskey getaway en route.

2 When I visited, the whiskey pot stills had not yet arrived, so you will see some of the newest stills on the island.

3 Gin fans will appreciate the efforts put forth in sourcing local botanicals and finding just the right person to help them narrow down the list.

MORE INFORMATION: *whiskey-lore.com/skellig*

Waterford Distillery

ABOUT WATERFORD DISTILLERY

If you are a lover of science, this is the distillery for you. When Mark Reynier left Islay in Scotland for a new adventure, world-renowned Irish barley was at the top of his mind. In 2015, he purchased a historic 18th-century brewery and built a state-of-the-art, automated distillery. The team's focus was working with farms across the island to develop a grand experiment in taste, asking the question how much impact does terrior have on whisky? With the distillery opening up to visitors, now is the time to learn.

The tour is a pleasant mix of science, innovation, and history. You begin with a view of their century-old mash tuns and the facility that has produced beer since the 1790s. Then step into the beautiful gardens, where you can walk inside a Scottish pot still that, in the past, distilled both Waterford and Bruichladdich whiskies. Now comes the science as they introduce you to the unique way the team sources their barley, keeps it separated throughout the process, and then uses the information they gather to create cuvées and special farm editions of their whisky.

At every distillery you visit, there are nuances to learn about the distilling process. At Waterford, be prepared to have your knowledge supercharged. Nothing will capture your imagination more than when you taste the spirits and learn about the blending of flavor profiles. This is truly one of the most unique distillery experiences in the world.

LISTEN/WATCH FOR

To focus specifically on the flavors and characteristics of an individual farm's barley, other elements of the distilling process need to be consistent from batch to batch. Listen to see if you can pick out which elements don't change from distillation to distillation.

GETTING THERE

Parking is limited on-site; your best bet is to park in town and walk to the distillery.

BASIC TOUR

Monday through Friday

SIDE TRIPS

- **House of Waterford Crystal Guided Factory Tour** Get a chance to see how world-famous Waterford Crystal is made in this behind-the-scenes tour.
- **Waterford Treasures Medieval Museum** Learn the history of Waterford and old world Ireland going back to the Vikings

CLOSEST DISTILLERIES

- **Ballykeefe Distillery** (N-52 km)
- **Blackwater Distillery** (W-79 km)

At A Glance

BRAND	Waterford
WHISKEY	Single Malt
FIRST BARREL FILLED	2015
AVAILABLE TO TOUR	Milling, Fermenters, Pot Still
TOUR COST	€€€
WEBSITE	*waterfordwhisky.com*
LOCATION	9 Mary St, Grattan Quay, Waterford City, Co. Waterford, X91 KF51, Ireland

Drew's Top Three Reasons to Visit

1 Many distilleries talk about the science of distilling, but here you will feel like you are getting your PhD. Waterford's process of discovering flavors through distillation goes well beyond any distillery I have ever visited. Science was never my strong suit, but here, the marriage between whisky and flavor makes it fascinating.

2 Tucked away on the waterfront, it is amazing to think how much distillery they have packed into such a small space—from the historic old brewery to the gardens and multi-level production area.

3 If you are a fan of Guinness, you will enjoy seeing the old brewery equipment. The beer giant acquired this facility in the 1950s and put a lot of money into its renovation. Several employees of the current distillery worked at this same location when it was a brewery.

MORE INFORMATION: *whiskey-lore.com/waterford*

SOUTH

South Considerations

BLACK'S OF KINSALE

A project that was announced as I started my travels around Ireland is a new Black's of Kinsale Distillery and Brewery, near the banks of the River Bandon. Husband and wife team Sam and Maudeline Black will celebrate ten years in business in 2023 with this new facility. They are sourcing their current selection of whiskeys, but have been distilling their own in-house spirits for some time, including an Irish rum. The new facility will help increase the production of their whiskeys and bring a great visitors' attraction to the foodie town of Kinsale. Estimated opening in 2023.

FEATURED BRAND	Black's
WHISKEYS+	Pot Still, Single Malt, Blend, Gin, Rum
TOURS	TBD (check website for updates)
WEBSITE	*blacksbrewery.com/spirits*

KILLARNEY DISTILLERY (TORC BREWING)

This is not a misprint. At the moment there are two distilleries in Killarney that bear the town's name. And while there are similarities in name, these are distilleries that are worlds apart in terms of size and style. Torc Brewing owners Aiden Forde and John Keane have ambitious plans to integrate different styles of distilling into different communities around the area. To show the level of creativity here, despite having already been to several distilleries that customized their stills, this was the first I visited that built their own still from scratch. I also saw the most oddly shaped oak barrel I have ever come across, which they had coopered themselves out of fallen Irish oak trees. They are also setting themselves apart by growing their own barley, doing floor maltings, and fermenting on-grain. Transparency is a major focus for Aiden and John and they are staunch advocates of honoring the town by providing a local product.

Located just north of Killarney, they not only brew and distill, they also roast coffee and make some delicious chocolates. Aiden and John are truly fascinating people, and it will be fun watching their plans unfold. If you are interested in a tour, your best bet is to reach out to the distillery through their social media.

FEATURED BRAND	TBD
WHISKEYS+	Pot Still, Single Malt, Blend, Poitín, Rum, Gin
FIRST BARREL FILLED	2021
TOURS	Ask
WEBSITE	*killarneywhisky.ie*

ROYAL OAK DISTILLERY

When the Italian drinks company Disaronno looked to expand its portfolio into the world of whiskey, it was their feeling that the growing reputation of the Irish spirit made it the perfect match for their brands. The distillery is in the breadbasket of Ireland: when you walk into the distillery you pass beautiful oak trees, water, and barley. The goal is to create a portfolio of whiskeys using 100% Irish grain. To that end, they have shifted their grain whiskey production over to using native wheat and barley. The Busker is one of the few Irish whiskeys that is made completely in-house, thanks to their on-site column stills. They produce a single malt, single pot still, grain whiskey, and a triple blend.

This is a great facility to visit. However, since the pandemic, they have put their focus on distilling and moved away from giving tours. That said, when planning your trip around Ireland, check out the website to see if things have changed. It is a great distillery to tour if you can.

FEATURED BRAND	The Busker
WHISKEYS	Pot Still, Single Malt, Grain, Blend
FIRST BARREL FILLED	2016
TOURS	TBD (check website for updates)
WEBSITE	*royaloakdistillery.com*

TIPPERARY DISTILLERY

Imagine finishing up a distillery tour and enjoying whiskey samples outdoors while watching barley wave in the breeze. That is the future the Tipperary Boutique Distillery envisions. The project started when Liam Ahearn, a fifth-generation farmer, met Scottish accountant Jennifer Nickerson. Jennifer's father Stuart, a scotch whisky industry veteran, saw great potential in using the Ahearn grain for production of Irish whiskey. Jennifer, Liam, and Stuart have now built a distillery and are laying down casks for your future enjoyment.

This distillery provides the ability for a true grain-to-glass experience. Wheat, oats, and barley stand right outside the door. Inside, electric Portuguese stills provide the distillation power, and the site bottles its own whiskey and contracts for others. Every bit of the process is tracked using a QR code system. This will allow for a high level of transparency with every bottle. Their own grain has been distilled off-site since 2017. Distilling on-site began in 2020.

The names of their whiskeys will speak to how and where they were distilled: Tipperary Boutique is the sourced whiskey; Tipperary is their grain distilled off-site; and the Tipperary Distillery brand will encompass the future on-site distilled brand. They are planning for future tours and tastings, so check their website to see if these have started in time for your trip.

FEATURED BRANDS	Tipperary Boutique, Tipperary
WHISKEYS+	Blended, Pot Still, Single Malt, Gin
FIRST BARREL FILLED	2017 (from farm grain) 2020 (on-site distilled)
TOURS	TBD (check website for updates)
WEBSITE	*tipperarydistillery.ie*

WAYWARD IRISH SPIRITS

From the front porch of Lakeview House & Estate is a wonderful view of Lough Leane, with the incredible mountain range of Killarney National Park right behind it. Whiskey might not be the first thing on your mind when you see it, but just behind the house there is a warehouse filled with barrels of aging spirits. This is the home of Sir Maurice O'Connell, a man whose family has a history of legal trade and illegal smuggling. He is also a descendant of one of Ireland's great heroes, Daniel O'Connell. Known to many as The Liberator, O'Connell was the leader who helped bring Irish Catholics emancipation after centuries of oppression.

Maurice's whiskeys are currently distilled off-site, but grains used in its distillation come directly from the estate. After distillation, they return to the estate and are aged in a bonded farm building using high-quality tawny and ruby port casks. While there is a building that could house stills in the future, there are no immediate plans for tour experiences. For now, they reserve it for special events.

FEATURED BRANDS	The Liberator, Lakeview Single Estate
WHISKEYS	Malt, Blend
TOURS	TBD (not currently planned)
WEBSITE	*waywardirish.com*

WEST CORK DISTILLERY

The amazing thing about West Cork is how the distillery came together. Three friends started in a garage and sourced spare parts from other industrial sites and distilleries. From there, they have built an impressive facility in Skibbereen. And not only does West Cork distill their own brand, they also provide sourced whiskey for many of Ireland and Northern Ireland's startup craft distilleries.

A tour of this facility is fascinating, with a real behind-the-scenes kind of feel. It seems that no part of the facility is off-limits and they are transparent about their processes. That said, they do not advertise tours, though they are happy to walk guests around at certain points during the day. If you are going to be in the area, your best bet is to contact the distillery directly, to see if they can accommodate you.

FEATURED BRAND	West Cork
WHISKEYS+	Pot Still, Single Malt, Blend, Grain, Vodka, Gin
FIRST BARREL FILLED	2003
TOURS	Ask
WEBSITE	*westcorkdistillers.com*

Appendix: Brand Index

BRAND	DISTILLERY
Athrú	Lough Gill
Ardara	Ardara
Ballyhoo	Connacht
Ballykeefe	Ballykeefe
Bart's	Lough Ree
Black's	Black's of Kinsale
Blue Spot	Midleton
Burke's	Great Northern Distillery
Bushmills	Bushmills
Busker, The	Royal Oak
Clan Colla	Ahascragh
Clonakilty	Clonakilty
Connacht	Connacht
Connemara	Kilbeggan
Cooper, The	Nephin
Croithlí	Crolly
Currach	Jim Beam
Dead Rabbit, The	Dublin Liberties
Dingle	Dingle
Dirtgrain	Blackwater
Drumshanbo	Shed, The
Dublin Liberties	Dublin Liberties
Dubliner, The	Dublin Liberties
Dunville's	Echlinville
Feckin	Echlinville
Fercullen	Powerscourt
Glendalough	Glendalough
Green Spot	Midleton

BRAND	DISTILLERY
Hinch	Hinch
IrishAmerican	Achill Island
Jameson	Midleton
Kilbeggan	Kilbeggan
Killarney	Killarney (Brewing & Distilling)
Killowen	Killowen
Lakeview Single Estate	Wayward Irish Spirits
Liberator, The	Wayward Irish Spirits
Limavady	Limavady
Lír	Glens of Antrim
Loch Measc	Lough Mask
Lough Ree	Lough Ree
Matt D'Arcy	Echlinville
May Lóag	Old Carrick Mill
Merchant Quay	Copeland's
McConnell's	J&J McConnell's
Method and Madness	Midleton
Michael Collins	Lough Gill
Micil	Micil
Midleton	Midleton
Mulroy Bay	Baoileach
Old Comber	Echlinville
Paddy's	Lough Gill
Pearse	Pearse Lyons
Powers	Midleton
Redbreast	Midleton
Roe & Co.	Roe & Co.
Shortcross	Rademon Estate
Silkie	Ardara
Skellig Six18	Skellig Six18

BRAND	DISTILLERY
Slane	Slane
Sliabh Liag	Ardara
Spade & Bushel	Connacht
Teeling	Teeling
Tipperary	Tipperary
Titanic	Titanic
Tullamore D.E.W.	Tullamore D.E.W.
Tyrconnell	Kilbeggan
Uais	Ahascragh
Waterford	Waterford
West Cork	West Cork
Whistler, The	Boann
Velvet Cap	Blackwater
Yellow Spot	Midleton

Other brands without immediately planned distilleries: Clontarf 1014, Currach, Egan's, Flaming Pig, Foxes Bow, Gelston's, Grace O'Malley, Hyde, The Irishman, JJ Corry, Kinahan's, Kirker & Greer, Knappogue Castle, Lambay, Natterjack, O'Driscolls, Pogues, Proclamation, Proper No. Twelve, Quiet Man, Sadler's, Sailor's Home, Sexton, Two Stacks, Writer's Tears

Acknowledgements

THANKS TO:

My Whiskey Lore family, especially those fiercely loyal Patreon members who have been here from the beginning. I treasure your friendship and support. Thank you Fernando Rivera, Todd Ritter, Robert Dixon, Ron Montgomery, Matthew King, Nick Streeter, Mike Hanson, Dean Dawsett, and Matt Kirkpatrick.

All of the amazing friends, family, and followers who support me on Facebook, Instagram, YouTube, and on both Whiskey Lore podcasts.

Emma Gibbs for the yeoman's job you did in brushing up my text, removing inconsistencies, and providing helpful suggestions along the way. It is always a pleasure working with you.

Michael Boalch for coming through in a pinch after my previous designer disappeared in the middle of the project. I appreciate your easy going way and the speed and focus you gave to the project.

The tour guides, brand ambassadors and owners from each of the distilleries I visited throughout Ireland and Northern Ireland. Your love and passion for your whiskey and Irish whiskey as a whole is inspiring. Thank you for sharing your love of stories, history, and amazing spirits.

Sláinte!

-Drew Hannush

Bibliography

BOOKS

- Barnard, Alfred. *The Whisky Distilleries of the United Kingdom*, Birlinn Ltd. (Reprint 2008)
- Given, Patrick. *Calico to Whiskey - A Case Study on the Development of the Distilling Industry NAAS 1700-1921*. Doctoral Thesis. Department of History, National University of Ireland-Maynooth. (August 2011)
- Mulryan, Peter, *The Whiskeys of Ireland*, The O'Brien Press; 2nd edition (October 8, 2016)
- O'Connor, Fionnán, *A Glass Apart: Irish Single Pot Still Whiskey*, Images Publishing Group (June 5, 2017)

There Is More For You

DISCOVER MORE ABOUT WHISKEYS
AROUND THE WORLD IN THREE EASY STEPS

Join the Whiskey Lore Society and get exclusive content,
access to a growing list of distilleries,
and alerts about upcoming events.

Get travel and whiskey inspiration daily.
Be a part of the conversation at *facebook.com/whiskeylore*
and *instagram.com/whiskeylore*.

Learn about whiskey history, myths, and legends by subscribing
to the *Whiskey Lore Stories Podcast* on your favorite podcast app.
Season Six is all about Irish whiskey.

START TODAY

Say "YES" to joining the Whiskey Lore Society:

whiskey-lore.com/signup

Make sure to use the promo code "**withorwithoute**" to get FREE access
to the online distillery guide, wish list feature, brand-to-distillery index
and to sign up for the *Whiskey Lore Society Newsletter*.

Can You Do Me A Favor?

THANK YOU FOR READING MY BOOK!

I really appreciate all of your feedback,
and I love hearing what you have to say.

I need your input to make the next version of this book
and my future travel guides better.

Please leave me an honest review on Amazon,
letting me know what you thought of the book.

Thanks so much!

Drew Hannush

Made in the USA
Middletown, DE
24 February 2023

25507164R00097